Relationship Banking

CROSS-SELLING
the Bank's Products & Services to Meet
Your Customer's Every Financial Need

Dwight S. Ritter

BANKERS PUBLISHING COMPANY
PROBUS PUBLISHING COMPANY
Chicago, Illinois
Cambridge, England

New Publications Bulletin

ISBN 1-55738-381-2

Printed in the United States of America

BB

CTV/BJS

1 2 3 4 5 6 7 8 9 0

In loving memory of Boy F. Dog

CONTENTS

PREFACE

I wrote the first version of this book several years ago, in 1987. I had spent the previous seventeen years consulting with community banks throughout the U.S., assisting in the development of a sales culture. I had garnered a great deal of experience sitting at desks in lobbies of retail banks, selling to the average customer. I had been a teller, managed a few banks, and created marketing plans and programs for several banks. (Actually, it was 635 banks by 1987.) Readers of my first book recognized that I had a lot of practical experience on the front line, rather than an academic, hands-off approach. So my book was very successful. By the early '90s, however, the retail banking industry had changed so much that much of the content was out-of-date.

What kind of changes?

- Slow loss of market share for Certificates of Deposit.
- Fluctuation of interest rates between 18 and 7 percent.
- Tightening, then re-defining, of credit requirements.
- Slowing of new car sales.

- Increase in credit card usage.
- Introduction of mutual funds.
- Growth in competition—product-wise and service-wise.
- Changing of management attitudes from uncontrolled growth to controlled growth and profits.
- Sophistication of total computer technology within the industry.

I also had learned a lot during the turn of the decade and early '90s. My consultancy expanded to include many international banks, private banks, mutual funds, law firms and accounting firms. I began to see how these many products and services were related to each other; how these were endless opportunities from a sales and marketing point of view to improve profits.

I had learned that the second product is much easier to sell than the first product, that the emphasis should be put on servicing existing customers and cross-selling, rather than creating new customers.

Most important, I had developed a sensitivity to the "tone" of a financial services sales environment. Witnessing and participating in many sales encounters had taught me how to walk that thin line between providing information (on one side) and asking for the order (on the other side). That delicate walk must be executed in a low-key, professional manner. It is Soft-Selling in its most sophisticated expression.

So this book will teach you exactly how to sell financial products and services from a soft-sales point of view.

It will teach you how to sell products and services "off-of" other related financial products and services.

It will teach you how to sell when there are ten people waiting for you—and how to sell when there are no other customers in the bank (we call this "Tuesday" selling versus "Thursday" selling).

This book will also teach you how to conduct the kind of sales encounter where the customer does the talking and you do the listening.

So, with the help of some great editing assistance and patience on the part of the publisher, we restructured my old book, broadening it to include the primary service influences on retail banking, and we broadened the product knowledge to include many international financial and fiduciary products and services. We also focused this book more on techniques and how-to and eliminated much of the theory. We felt this was more appropriate to the leaner, meaner '90s.

This book is divided into four sections. The first is background, illustrating how the industry has changed and why its employees have had to change. The second section is hard-core sales techniques. The third section explains the inter-relationship of products and services within the industry. The fourth section presents a few case studies—realistic dialogue taking place in realistic situations.

I am very pleased with how this book has evolved. For those readers who bought my first book, *Cross-Selling Financial Services*, this book is different. It is much more hands-on, presenting more techniques and reflecting more practical situations. You will find this book is a complete, well-researched guide for today's retail banker.

Section ONE

Background

Chapter ONE

THE CHANGING WORLD OF FINANCIAL AND FIDUCIARY SERVICES

The world of financial services is not what it was twenty years ago, ten years ago, or even two years ago.

Financial services and their companions, fiduciary services, have expanded enormously of late and the impact of that expansion on banking has been explosive.

Selling these services, and most important of all, cross-selling them, are the "hot" keys to success in banking.

It's my intention to tell you how to use those keys to your bank's best advantage. So, let's start at the beginning and take a brief look at what fiduciary and financial services comprise.

The word "fiduciary" has only recently emerged into fairly common American usage and so it tends to be confusing. You can look it up in several dictionaries and come away with several vaguely differing definitions, complicated by the fact that fiduciary is both a noun (a person), and an adjective (describing the duties of that person). These definitions, then, might include a trustee, of or pertaining to a trust, the legal holder of a trust, etc. Internationally, a fiduciary (the person) is expected to have legal and tax expertise and fiduciary responsibility is of great importance and commands considerable respect.

For our purposes, I'll break down fiduciary services as those focusing on:

1. Protection and control of one's assets

2. Confidentiality of one's investments

3. Minimization of tax vulnerability.

Actual products fitting into this category are trusts, jurisdictional corporate law, international tax treaties, accounting, and legal assistance (related to investment management).

Financial services on the other hand focus more sharply on:

1. Preservation and enhancement of capital

2. Protection of assets

3. Access to capital.

To put the emergence of financial and fiduciary services into a loose historical perspective, let's look at the late 1940s when financial services in banking consisted of checking accounts (mostly corporate), savings accounts and mortgages. Loans were not the common product they are today. Credit cards were issued by "departments stores and gas stations." Wealthy individuals increased their wealth (or tried to) by dealing with brokers. There were some private banks back then, content to remain largely anonymous, known only to the very wealthy they had served with a mix of financial and fiduciary services from generation to generation . . . with some relationships in Europe dating back hundreds of years.

The financial services business remained fairly simple for the next couple of decades. Yes, bank branches sprang up in city and suburbs, toasters and other items were offered to attract new customers, personal checking accounts became more common, but the product base remained much the same.

Then came the '70s with bank deregulation, the advent of mutual funds and supply side economics effecting substantive changes in the general financial services environment. Certificates of Deposit were introduced and with increasing acceleration were replaced in the '80s by stock and bond mutual funds as the way for banks to hold onto customers. In the '90s, the traditional retail bank has been forced to develop more investment products just to retain present clients and make their relationships profitable. The traditional bank customer-service employee is becoming a thing of the past. Now that employee must think about account relationships rather than products. If he or she doesn't, the customer will leave in search of a better relationship.

Cross-selling financial and fiduciary services has become the best method for building account relationships, holding existing customers and creating a more profitable customer relationship—for the financial institution and for the customer.

Let's explore a case in point: A 45-year-old business executive comes to open a personal checking account. Ten years ago, most retail bankers only looked at that client as, "a checking account." Today's financial services salesperson, with the bank's profits in mind, looks at that client as a potential melding of several products based on the client's individual needs.

The task, then, is to determine the needs. The cross-sales could be:

1. An ATM card
2. Direct payroll deposit to checking/savings
3. Overdraft protection
4. Automatic deductions from checking
5. Either a CD or mutual fund
6. IRA
7. Mortgage
8. Insurance
9. Installment loans
10. Brokerage services.

If the new customer is connected to the right kind of business additional possible cross-sales include:

11. Business checking
12. Automatic payroll processing
13. Cash management services
14. Pension fund administration
15. Commercial loans
16. Accounting
17. Limited legal services.

And, finally, if the client's business is international, even more cross-sales can be developed, such as:

18. Foreign sales corporations for exporters
19. Creation of offshore management services
20. Accounting and limited legal advice concerning overseas business.

All of those services could be related, depending on the client's needs, but theoretically our business executive working for a large corporation (or import/exporter) presents at least 20 service-relationship opportunities. But, most important here, we've introduced the concept of using the need for one product to create the need for other related products. That concept is called Relationship Selling.

Those 20 services can make that one consumer checking account extremely profitable!

Of course, cross-selling has been used in the banking industry for the past ten years with widely varying degrees of success and intensity. But many bankers still have difficulty conceptualizing that they should actually sell other services to their clients. They seemingly prefer to wait for their clients to ask for additional services.

It's my contention, and one of my prime reasons for writing this book, that the reluctance to sell can be overcome through practical application of the proven sales theory and techniques I am about to describe.

HIGH KNOWLEDGE/HIGH RISK VERSUS LOW KNOWLEDGE/LOW RISK

Selling a broad range of financial services requires a very thorough understanding of many products and services plus the understanding of many different kinds of businesses and trusts. Perhaps the thorough understanding of all services would be too difficult. That is why the financial services industry comprises specialty groups like retail banks, trust companies, insurance companies, mutual funds, commercial banks, stock brokerages, law firms, and accounting firms.

Some financial services are extremely complicated: annuities or international tax issues, net lease investments, junk bonds, etc. Others are simpler: checking, savings, etc. Yet some of the complex services (like legal services) are easy to sell. Conversely some very simple services are difficult to sell (like business checking accounts). Figure 1.1 illustrates four quadrants comparing the varying degrees of product knowledge versus sales knowledge. It also illustrates those products/services which are considered difficult to sell, as well as difficult to understand.

There are so many financial services today that the very idea of knowing enough to sell several is intimidating. The answer, of course, is to specialize yet broaden your knowledge of the overall industry as much as possible—from a general point of view.

SALES ARE "UNGENTLEMANLY"

The growth in the number and variety of financial and fiduciary products and services has intensified competition greatly and made a thorough knowledge of marketing and sales essential. Those individuals in the traditional financial and fiduciary services business who are uncomfortable with the idea of selling often feel that selling means forcing a service on a customer. The image of the sales person is not the image that they would choose for themselves. Financial and fiduciary services providers cultivate a self-image of professionalism much like physicians or attorneys. In their view salespeople sell used cars and gold watches, wear loud sport jackets and talk loud and fast.

Over the years most cultures have been influenced by media handling of the image of the salesperson. *Death of a Salesman* and many other books and movies have depicted a person—a *sales*person, drummer, commercial traveler—in a very negative light. A British acquaintance of mine regards selling as "ungen-

Figure 1.1

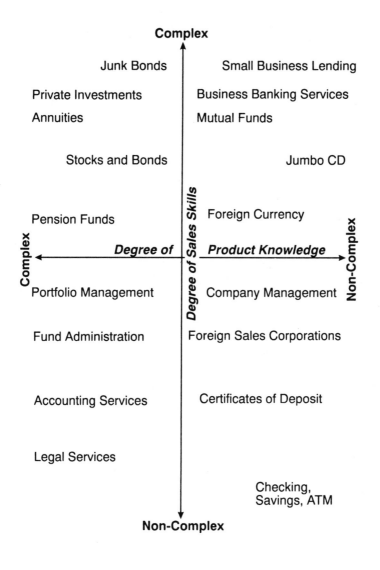

tlemanly." People generally do not have a favorable impression of selling.

I have been doing sales training in financial institutions for over twenty years and some time ago I began opening each seminar by asking the participants to give me adjectives that best describe sales people. The following list seems to cover most of the feelings:

aggressive	pushy	intimidating
dishonest	opportunistic	vulgar
sleazy	hyped	fast-talking
evasive	shifty	manipulative
insincere	gross	tense

Aggressive and opportunistic seem to be the most favorable epithets here. That perceived negative imaging frequently discourages bankers from seeing themselves in sales. And, they can project themselves as being rejected, an unpleasant situation.

This self-conscious view conflicts with the necessity of being proactive in generating new business. They need to be convinced that selling is integral to the service delivery system and is essential to proper job performance. They have to realize that there is more competition, more companies offering the same service. And that means they have to revamp their view of sales and salespeople.

EVERYONE SELLS

Selling *IS* an honorable profession. Priests and ministers are salespeople. They are selling ideas. We buy those ideas, and we act on them. Since we fund clerical salaries we even pay for the ideas.

Doctors are salespeople. One goes into their offices with a problem. They ask questions and tell you what you need. Dentists, too, sell. The last time I visited my dentist, after he had cleaned my teeth, he commented on how much better I would look if the false tooth I have in the front were replaced with a new one. He was selling and I was buying.

City planners are salespeople selling their ideas to a community. Architects must sell prospective clients on the merits of their firm. Perhaps the closest profession to the traditional description of financial services is lawyers. They *sell* legal services. You are buying.

It's just that doctors are called doctors, dentists are called dentists, ministers are called ministers and so on. Unfortunately Willie Loman, the protagonist in *Death of a Salesman* was called a salesman!

HARD-SELLING VERSUS SOFT-SELLING

If you have ever gone to a "friendly breakfast to learn about a time-shared condominium" you know what hard-selling is. And if you have ever gone to a dentist for a cleaning (and buy dental floss, sign up for two cleanings per year, and get some bonding on your crooked front tooth)—you know what soft-selling is.

Who are hard-sellers and who are soft-sellers? Most automobile sales personnel are hard-sellers, as are most time-shared condominium sales people, door to door encyclopedia vendors, and vacuum cleaner sales people. Many realtors, family counseling centers, established stock brokers, some life insurance and financial institutions tend toward soft-selling.

One of the major differences between hard-selling and soft-selling is where the emphasis (or greatest concentration of intensity) lies. Figure 1.2 is a simplified graph that illustrates the various stages of an average sales process.

- Pre-Approach Planning
- Introduction
- Needs Analysis
- Needs Fulfillment
- Close
- Follow up

Those six steps are on the horizontal axis and the commensurate levels of intensity are on the vertical axis. The level of intensity can best be defined as the amount of time that one would spend on certain parts of the sales process. It also reflects importance that we place on certain parts of the sales process.

Let's follow the dotted line first. It represents the intensity of the Hard-Sell process. In the beginning of a Hard-Sell, the most important psychological ingredient is nerve! The Hard-Sell salesperson introduces him or herself, shakes everyone's hand and refers to everyone by their first name. A good Hard-Sell salesperson brags that he or she can sell anything. They don't have to know a lot about the product. All they have to do is take charge and control the tempo. That is why the dotted line starts out low on the intensity scale. The introduction is important to the Hard-Sell salesperson, as is an over-simplified understanding of the concept of needs analysis. For example, a Hard-Sell salesperson (an automobile salesperson) feels that the customer's sole need is a car. It's that simple (and quite wrong).

At the Needs Fulfillment stage the hard-seller loses interest (because satisfying the needs of a customer might mean not

Figure 1.2

Sales Emphasis by Type of Selling

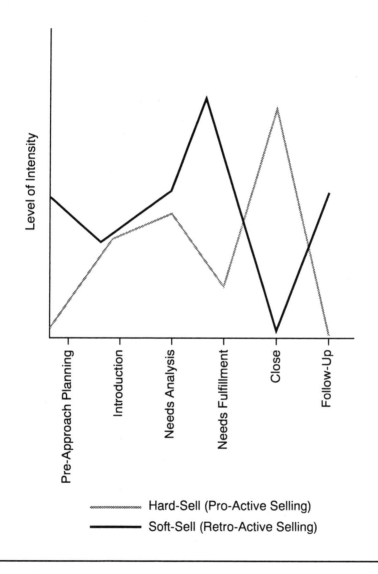

closing the sale). So the Hard-Sell salesperson skims over this step. Now comes the close. That is where hard-selling concentrates. The salesperson starts closing the sale the minute he walks up to you. In a car lot, for example, the salesperson wants to know if you are looking or buying. They will ask you precisely that question. If you're "just looking," they are not interested. Their closing techniques utilize time. That means there is always something that will negate the offer if the customer doesn't buy right away.

A Soft-Sell salesperson would be very interested if the customer were "just looking" because they are cultivating a relationship rather than just closing a sale. As far as a follow-up is concerned the Hard-Salesperson is more concerned about the next customer. There's an old expression in the automobile sales business, "Either buy or fly!"

Now the solid line is the Soft-Sales process. Pre-Approach planning is very important. A thorough knowledge of the product and how it satisfies the needs of various kinds of customers is paramount. The Introduction is still important. But, with the Soft-Salesperson, the Needs Analysis begins to take on a more important role because the salesperson must find out the kinds of needs that have created the curiosity about the product. And the Needs Fulfillment is the most important part of a Soft- Salesperson's job: Matching products to needs. If the customer doesn't need the product, don't sell it. The close is almost incidental. If the customer feels that the product is going to satisfy his or her need, they will ask for the order or welcome the suggestion of purchase.

And, finally, the Follow-up: Allowing some time to pass, then calling the customer back, sending relevant information by mail and, in general, further cultivating the relationship. As you can see, from a momentum point of view, there is a big difference between Hard-Selling and Soft-Selling. The biggest difference lies in the closing techniques. When you are an internal salesperson for a financial institution you should not have to rely on asking for the order to make the sale. If you have done your job in terms of addressing the customer's needs, the order will be requested by the customer. Or you might have to say something like, "It seems that this product does everything you are interested in. Don't you agree?"

Soft-Sellers concentrate on the customer—not on the sale. That is basically a behavioral theory of winning. If you think a lot about how you are going to pay your bills, you will have difficulty making a lot of money. The same thing applies to thinking a lot about making the sale. If you become obsessed with "selling" and making multiple sales on each customer you will end up wondering why those customers don't come back and ask for you. In selling financial services, repeat customers are the key. If you push, you will push the customer away from you . . . and away from your financial institution. You should be concentrating on cultivating a relationship with your customer rather than selling a product. That does not mean that you are no longer accountable for multiple sales. However, if you address yourself to the needs of every customer, you will find success in selling, as well as a personal feeling of fulfillment.

Addressing the needs of your customer in the Soft-Sell is a skill in itself. It involves the disciplined study of interpersonal communication as it is applicable to sales. The next chapter will begin this study.

SUMMARY

1. Fiduciary services focus on asset protection and control, the confidentiality of investments, and minimization of tax vulnerability.

2. Some typical fiduciary services are trusts, jurisdictional corporate law, international tax treaties, accounting, and legal assistance (related to investment management).

3. Financial services focus on capital preservation and enhancement, asset protection, and access to capital.

4. Some typical traditional financial services include checking, savings, loans and time deposits.

5. Relationship selling involves using the need for one product to create the need for other related products.

6. Our concept of "sales" has been negatively conditioned by the exaggerations of such characters as Willie Loman and stereotyped by the plaid sports-jacketed used car salesman. Consequently, selling is not perceived as a noble profession.

7. Hard-Selling concentrates on closing the sale and moving on to the next customer. Hard-Selling is not sensitive to the real needs of the customer.

8. Soft-Selling concentrates on the needs of the customer and relies on the fact that if those needs are satisfied, the customer will close the sale.

9. The six parts of a Sales Process are Pre-Approach Planning, Introduction, Needs Analysis, Needs Fulfillment, Close, and Follow up.

Section TWO

Selling Techniques

Chapter TWO

COMMUNICATION

Understanding financial services is very important, but understanding the customer is even more important. In the financial services industry the objective should only be to provide those products and services that our customers really need. That requires acquiring communication skills first and then absorbing product knowledge.

Understanding how humans talk to each other—and what they are really saying—is crucial. Communication demands reading other people, reacting to them appropriately, controlling situations, and, most critical, making people feel comfortable around you.

MAKING PEOPLE COMFORTABLE AROUND YOU

I have a friend who is a minister. Once we were talking and he asked, "Dwight, what do you really want out of life?" I thought about that for awhile. What did I really want out of life? Money? Peace of mind? What?

If I won the lottery, would I be totally happy? I thought that over briefly and knew I would be happy, but that I'd rather have something "deeper" as well. I need some sense of accomplishment. Luck does not offer a great sense of accomplishment.

I want to be successful and happy. I can't imagine I could be happy without being successful. Successful doesn't necessarily mean making lots of money. Successful means—well—successful in my dealings with other people, because if I am successful there, then I will get what I want. If I am honest and sincere about what I want from other people, then I will achieve an inner sense of satisfaction. I will feel good because they feel good.

So, I answered my minister friend by saying, "I want to make people feel comfortable around me."

People who have mastered the art of making others feel at ease around them are people who are well liked, successful, and content. They are people committed to communication and to getting along with others, skills that are interrelated and, as you will see, eminently learnable.

INTERPERSONAL COMMUNICATION: THE THREE ELEMENTS

The concept of Interpersonal Communication can be simply defined as people communicating with each other. There are three very important parts of interpersonal communication:

1. Body language
2. Vocal tone
3. Words

Those three parts determine the effectiveness of communication. Communication is not just talking. It is talking and listening. It is how you appear when you are talking and how your voice sounds and what you are saying. Communication is also how you appear when you are listening, that is how you acknowledge the talker. Figure 2.1 illustrates the elements of personal communication.

Contrary to most people's beliefs, verbal communication (or words) is not the most important part of an overall communication. Actually they are the least important of the three. Research has shown us that the importance of words in the overall communication process is weighted at only 12 percent. Body language (or non-verbal communication) is the most dynamic of the three media, accounting for 55 percent of the total. The way we dress. The way we walk. How we sit, stand, lean, tilt our heads—all of that is the most important part of the total communication package.

And *how* you say those words is also very important. The tone of your voice. What your voice sounds like when you say things. Whiny, gruff, melodic, precise, monotonous. Do you whistle, sigh, grunt, stammer? This aspect of communication is said to make up 33 percent of the total.

So it isn't so much what you say as it is how you say it and how you appear when you are in the process of saying it. Even saying nothing is communication. How you appear as a listener affects your communication. The lesson here is not to overemphasize your words. Learn to look at the total package.

It's like an opera. You can follow and enjoy the performance, even if the opera is written in a language you don't understand. That's because the choreography (body language) and music (tone) predominate the communication package. The lyrics (words) trail in importance.

Figure 2.1

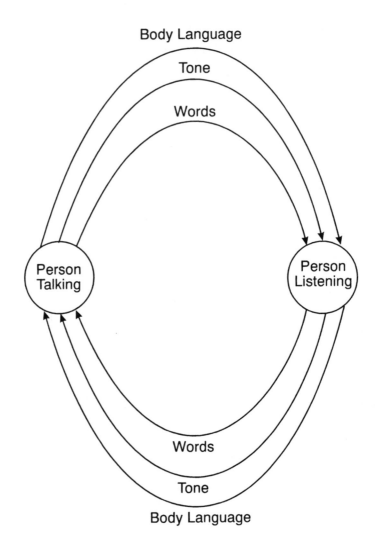

Of course, we are relating communication to selling: How well you sell depends on how well you know your customer; on how well you know yourself; and on how well you know your product. Most of all it depends on how well you communicate your knowledge.

You are the sum of the three communication elements as you talk and as you listen. The best sales people in the world are listeners. Selling is listening and assessing the needs of the customer; asking a few more questions to make sure you are right; then suggesting the right product to fit the needs. That process requires consummate communication skills, adeptness at talking, listening, and observation of non-verbal signals.

GETTING OFF TO THE RIGHT START

All communication has a starting point and an ending point. It is like a time line. A good communicator should be aware of the *communication time line*. You should learn to visualize this line in order to review a communication effort. Controlling the momentum of this time line is important. The most effective way to do that is: Always start the communication.

If you remember that rule, you will find that your customers will be reacting to your personality rather than you reacting to theirs. That concept is very important. Not only from the point of view of your job but also socially. An active communicator starts the communication, offers the hand first, introduces him or herself first, greets the customer first. Passive communicators wait for the customers to tell them what they want. If that is your style then you are reacting to your customer, from the very beginning.

Assess your sales environment. If you sit at a desk and customers come to you, the beginning of the communication is when you stand up to greet the customer. Standing up at your desk is a sign of professionalism. All business professionals stand up when someone approaches their desk. They do so because it shows respect for the customer and it is polite. Moreover, two people establish rapport best when their eyes are on a similar plane, i.e., two standing people, two sitting people, etc.

Eye-contact, coupled with a pleasant expression, is all-important. (Yes, it almost seems ridiculous to make that basic point, but I have watched bankers, stockbrokers, attorneys, financial planners, and insurance salespeople who, for one reason or another, do not establish and maintain eye-contact with the customer.)

So an effective communicator will establish eye-contact, then greet the customer by shaking his or her hand.

Then you speak. Whoever starts the communication—speaks first—is generally the person who is perceived (by virtue of the momentum) to be in charge of that communication. If you sit back and wait, you will become a pawn of your customer and struggle to become anything but an order-taker.

THREE STYLES OF COMMUNICATION

Eric Berne, a pioneer in the study of interpersonal communication and what he named Transactional Analysis, isolated three basic styles of communication: child, parent, and adult.

Having acknowledged my debt to Berne, I'm going to expand on his theory and apply it more specifically to sales and management. I'm even going to change the names of his style slightly to underscore their flexibility and frequent overlapping. I'm calling these styles: childlike, parentlike, adultlike. The chief traits of each of these behaviors can be described as follows:

Personality Styles in Transactional Analysis

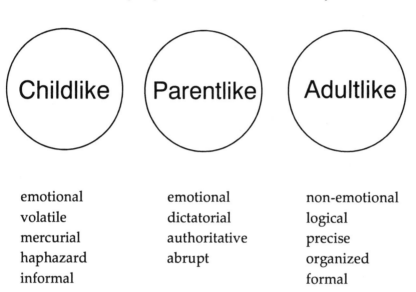

emotional	emotional	non-emotional
volatile	dictatorial	logical
mercurial	authoritative	precise
haphazard	abrupt	organized
informal		formal

Let's examine these behavioral styles in some more detail before we relate them to selling technique and to handling customers.

Childlike

Childlike behavior is evident in all ages and is characterized by extremes ranging from cuteness to lack of control. I'll use a personal example of cuteness—which in some circumstances can be very effective in securing one's way.

I recall my college-age daughter trying to wheedle me out of the use of a truck we own. She came to me with her hands clasped behind her, her lower lip puffed out slightly. She moved restlessly from foot to foot and tilted her head appealingly. She knew that I was prone to give into this type of behavior.

It is interesting that my initial response was just as childlike as hers. I used a pet name in addressing her and sort of whined about how the truck was needed to plow the driveway at home.

The chief point that I want to make here is that her childlike behavior evoked an immediate childlike reaction from me. That response is typical of childlike behavior. And that holds true at the other emotional extreme as well. The business manager who loses control simply spreads that lack of control, causing resistance among employees toward the very result that he or she is trying to achieve.

Two childlike humans carrying on a communication. One wants something and has set a goal for achieving it. The other is resisting albeit not very well.

Childlike behavior is two way behavior—one person talking with another person. One talking, another listening, then answering. Childlike behavior is emotional. It is informal, volatile, mercurial, impulsive, cutesy and laid-back.

Parentlike

This behavior usually seems ambiguous. At times, it appears almost unreasonable, even childlike. At other times it appears too reasonable—God-like, in a sense. It does frequently spark change.

In the exchange mentioned above I was acting childlike and so was my daughter. She was getting what she wanted. If I really wanted my truck then I should have realized that playing the game her way would never resolve the situation in my favor. So I should have changed the format. "Now you listen to me," I should have begun, and then gone on to tell her in very definite terms why it was totally necessary to keep the truck at home.

Parentlike communication is used a lot in business: The stern, abrupt order that must be followed or else. The large group tongue-lashing by the boss. It is emotional and unlike the other two styles it does not look for a dialogue. It only wants to be listened to, and have its orders followed. Parentlike communication is often encountered in situations where customers are unhappy, even angry. I'll cover this in more detail shortly.

Adultlike

Think of a business meeting in a spacious room with an oval table seating ten. Everyone is seated. Each has a file folder in front of them. There are two trays on which sit a water-filled glass pitcher surrounded by squeaky clean glasses turned upside-down.

You enter wearing a business suit and have a file folder tucked under your arm. The meeting is scheduled to begin at 9:00 a.m. It is 8:57 a.m.

You nod politely to everyone, and while arranging the contents of your folder into three neat files, chat briefly and quietly with the people sitting next to you.

Then you say pleasantly to the group, "Good morning. I've got three things I would like to cover today. First, the status of my negotiations with . . . "

You can sense the atmosphere. It is adultlike, a very effective behavior for meetings. It lends itself to productivity. Things tend to get done. Adultlike behavior is conducive to setting goals, giving out assignments and rules, setting deadlines, and budgets.

Adultlike communication is two-way communication, the same as childlike. But here one person communicates with another or others in adultlike fashion and elicits a similar response. Adultlike communication is non-emotional, formal, logical, precise and organized. Buttoned-up but not uptight.

DEALING WITH ANGER

If you deal with customers, even in the relatively dignified setting of banking, you're going to be dealing with anger and, as I've said, anger is parentlike behavior.

Many customers come into your bank believing that they have been wronged and they want you to make it right, even if that requires some groveling and apologizing on your part.

Learning to deal with angry customers is difficult and inhibits your ability to maintain the bank's relationship with them, much less to add to it, so an understanding of anger is important.

People show anger and impatience in different ways and the key to handling anger is to recognize it early. Our awareness that 88 percent of the total communication process is non-verbal should help us to recognize anger before it gets out of hand and even to halt conflict before it starts.

Here are some of the anger signals you should look for:

- folded arms
- lowered head
- clenched teeth
- abrupt head movements
- fast, deliberate walk
- noticeable fidgeting
- sighs

- resting on one foot, then the other
- crossing and un-crossing legs
- hands on hips
- constantly seeking eye contact
- narrowing of eyes
- exasperated expressions

These signs of impending conflict are familiar to all of us. Unfortunately, most of us react to them badly because we try to avoid conflict. We look the other way, avoiding eye-contact.

But the choice is not necessarily between fight and flight. If your goal is to minimize stress, flight is certainly the best alternative. However, minimizing stress and solving a problem are often in direct opposition. Just because a customer is angry does not mean you (personally) have made an error. All it means is that the customer is angry and it is your job to appease that anger. You are not wrong! You must simply realize that emotional parentlike behavior can be handled if you can understand anger.

First is the fact that most anger is cyclical in nature. It is an emotion looking for a solution. The path of the emotion is shown in Figure 2.2.

Actually, of course, a person may go through more than one anger cycle since the realization of appeasement can create anger, causing the cycle to repeat itself. And so it goes.

We cannot totally eliminate anger. We can appease it; maybe take some of it away. We should understand that all anger is looking for (1) someone or something to blame so that it can (2) demand justice and justice means some kind of (3) reward. The end of this emotional cycle is (4) relaxation, that "moment of truth" that comes from feeling that everything has been rectified.

Figure 2.2

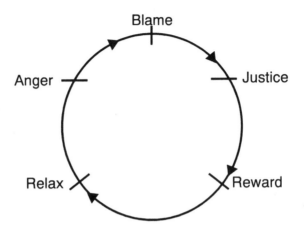

We can illustrate that cycle by using a retail banking setting: You are a customer. You have just been erroneously charged for overdrawing your bank account . . . for the fifth time! You are angry. Therefore (1) you want to find out who is to blame (2) so they will have to apologize and (3) tell you how good you are so you can (4) breath a sigh of relief that you were right all along.

Knowing that anger is a reward-seeking behavior and that it is parentlike in its demands, you can use this scenario to solidify a customer relationship and create a multiple product sale. How? By remembering that the best way to deal with parentlike anger is with adultlike behavior—the best way to deal with emotional behavior is with unemotional behavior. So matching a parentlike communication with an adultlike communication is conducive to problem resolution. Here is a simplified but proven approach toward resolving customer conflict to your advantage. When you are faced with an angry customer, try writing these letters on a piece of paper: L A E R. Here's what the letters stand for:

Listen.

Be extremely attentive. Establish eye contact. Become concerned and show it in your expression. Concentrate on what the customer is saying. Write it down.

Apologize.

As soon as the opportunity presents itself, apologize. Tell the customer you are sorry for any inconvenience. Remember: just because you say you are sorry it does not mean you personally are wrong—only that you are sorry. The word "sorry" implies that you are taking the blame—that justice has been served and the customer was right (for the sake of the argument). Tell the customer you will solve the problem while he or she is present.

Explore.

Now that the anger cycle has reached its end, you can begin getting to the real base of the problem. Determine in a quiet, logical way what happened that caused the anger. Do not try to find out what the customer did wrong so you can tell him or her.

Respond.

Now is the time that you can tell the customer what action you will be taking to solve the problem. Again, do not tell the customer he or she was wrong. . . even if that is the case. Your job is to solve the problem, not to prolong the argument.

And now the stage is set for some of the cross-selling techniques I'll be describing throughout this book. You've turned the crisis into opportunity.

Remember that handling conflict means understanding parentlike behavior. We know that the primary behavior for handling parentlike communication is adultlike. The alternative? Well, you could fall on your knees and beg forgiveness but I know you wouldn't do that.

SUMMARY

1. The three elements of communication, listed in order of weighted importance, are: Body language, 55 percent; tone of voice, 33 percent; words, only 12 percent.

2. The salesperson should always start the communication.

3. The three personality styles—child, parent, adult— were identified by Eric Berne in his pioneer research on interpersonal relations. Berne constructed the theory of Transactional Analysis.

4. Dealing with angry customers often means dealing with parentlike communication, which can be best countered with adultlike communication.

5. The cycle of anger is predictable and moves from

    (a) anger to

    (b) blame to

    (c) demand for justice to

    (d) reward to

    (e) relaxation.

6. When dealing with an angry customer, remember
    L A E R:
    Listen,
    Apologize,
    Explore,
    Respond.

Chapter THREE

THE FORMAL/INFORMAL CONTINUUM

In the previous chapter I mentioned Eric Berne's development of Transactional Analysis (TA). In this chapter I'm going to show you more specifically how to apply that theory to your selling technique.

Remember that Berne identified three categories of behavior: Childlike, Parentlike and Adultlike.

I found it easier and more practical to teach TA by eliminating parentlike behavior which is one-way communication, and not truly a communications behavior—more of a tool for understanding conflict. After doing that I asked my classes to give me just two adjectives that best described the remaining behaviors: childlike and adultlike. The adjectives advanced most frequently were, respectively, *informal* and *formal*.

I found it interesting that formal was the opposite of informal, just as childlike is the opposite of adultlike. It became apparent that it was even simpler to teach the practical use of TA by focusing on the formal-informal opposition. To do that, I developed the formal/informal continuum as illustrated in Figure 3.1.

Let's look at our Continuum more closely. On the far left side might be the most formal person you've met or heard of: Queen Elizabeth or Richard Nixon? The rigid Jim Dial in *Murphy Brown*, perhaps. Think for a while about how you might act around that type of formal behavior.

Now think about the most informal person you have ever heard of. Who is it? Rodney Dangerfield? Alan Alda? Will Rogers? Richard Pryor? How would you act around that person?

There's no denying that you would act differently around the formal people than the informal. That's because you instinctively adjust your behavior to that of the person with whom you are trying to communicate. It's natural. We do it until we become aware of it, then we decide whether we want to keep on doing it. But, we do adapt to someone else's personality.

The Formal/Informal Continuum Numbering System

A numbering system has been devised to assign comprehensible values to the varying degrees of formal and informal behavior. The system rated the most formal person (in our case, Queen Elizabeth) a 1, and the most informal person (Richard Pryor) a 10.

Figure 3.1

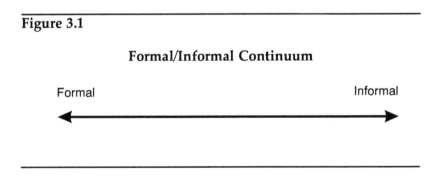

Formal/Informal Continuum

Formal   Informal

The numbering system made descriptions very easy. If Queen Elizabeth is a 1 (to the left of the continuum) and Richard Pryor is a 10 (to the right of the continuum) then where are you?

That numbering system has been studied and refined to determine that the most important number on the continuum was 5. Actually it was important to see how you perceived yourself acting as a 5. It was discovered that an effective salesperson could create an environment of trust and comfort quicker if he or she was not too far from the customer's continuum rating.

Figure 3.2

Formal/Informal Continuum

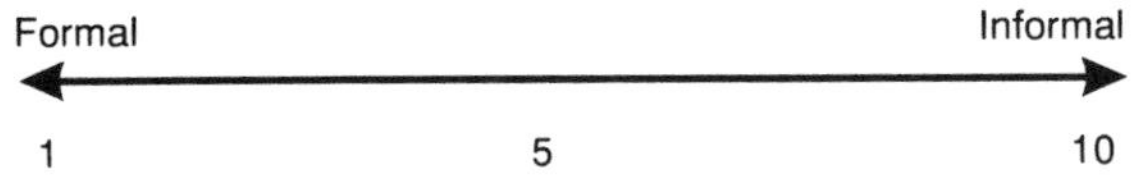

Formal   Informal

1   5   10

If the salesperson was a 7 and the customer was a 3, the difference between them is 4. It was actually determined that any difference higher than 3 was inhibiting the sales process because the customer would not be at a comfort level conducive to the kind of selling and cross-selling required in the financial services industry.

So, if the salesperson could clearly understand how to behave in order to be a 5, he could stay within three points of almost everyone. The difficult concept is to find your 5. Successful salespeople know exactly where their 5 is. They also know how to act in order to have a customer perceive them as a 5. To be a 5 is to be neutral and therefore able to move closer to your customer.

The idea then is to find out how to become more or less formal or informal. What are the characteristics that make up formal behavior? What constitutes informal behavior? In order to answer those questions accurately, we must return to our discussion of Body Language, Tone, and Voice in Chapter Two. We eventually understood that concept better as Choreography, Music, and Lyrics, Choreography and Music accounting for 88 percent of communication. Within each of those three categories there are characteristics that can be evaluated in terms of formal and informal. They are:

CHOREOGRAPHY

Physical Contact

Space

Posture

Gestures

Clothes Style

MUSIC

Rate

Volume

LYRICS

Language Selection

Topics

Organization

By grouping those ten characteristics into our three major categories, we can discuss each one within the weighted realm of the overall communications effort. As you read about these characteristics, you will discover that you might be very formal regarding some of them and very informal in others. But when you consider all ten of them (in the context of your own behavior), you

Figure 3.3

	CHOREOGRAPHY						MUSIC		LYRICS		
Communication Style	*Physical Contact*	*Space Limitations*	*Postures*	*Gestures*	*Clothes Style*	*Rate*	*Volume*	*Language Selection*	*Topics*	*Organization*
FORMAL (Adultlike)	Brief, firm handshake, avoids physical contact. Don't hug!	Needs large space. Keeps a distance from other people. Likes large rooms.	Closed rigid straight.	Few gestures. Deliberate and "jabbing" when used.	Neutral with high authority. Dark suits, etc.	Deliberate	Medium to loud	Many multi-syllable words. Specific, technical terms. Frequent use of business "buzz" words.	Accomplishment, performance	Primacy
INFORMAL (Childlike)	Lingering, "soft" handshakes. Back-patter. Hugger.	Needs very little space. Stands close when talking. Likes "cozy" little rooms.	Open relaxed, "S" shaped.	Many gestures aimless in nature. Lots of head movements.	Loose, unbuttoned. Leisure type. Loafers.	Medium to slow	Medium to soft	Many one syllable words. Many personal references. Sometimes vague or confusing. Lots of "in" dialogue. Slang.	Belonging. Confiding. Sharing.	Recency

will be either formal or informal. So you might decide you are very formal even though you do have some informal characteristics. Few people are totally formal or totally informal.

Choreography

Physical Contact. Formal people avoid unnecessary physical contact; hugging, for example. The more formal someone is, the less physical contact they prefer. Formal people prefer brief, firm handshakes. Quite logically, formal people, then, are uncomfortable around back patters and people who touch elbows while they are talking; guide them around a room physically; rest an arm on their shoulder, etc.

Socially some people hug when they greet. It is a sign of familiarity, of informality. But formal people are still uncomfortable with it. Socially it is acceptable (almost required, in many cultures) so formal people handle it non-emotionally.

It is important to note that physical contact as a mode of social communications is regulated by cultures. The French hug. They start each meeting with a handshake and end each meeting with a handshake. Close business associates will even start each day with a handshake. The Northern Europeans shake hands emotionally. Men and women kiss socially once in the US—three times in Europe (kissing a cheek just once in Europe is a sign of extreme familiarity). The Japanese avoid physical contact. They bow when introduced. The Russians embrace. Latins and Middle Easterners stand closer and are more touch oriented. They prefer limp handshakes. Strong Texas-like, pumping handshakes are a sign of physical confrontation. In Southeast Asia, the handshake is replaced by the wai. This practice involves putting ones palms together in front of the chest, like praying. No physical contact. It is best to observe customs in a country; to inquire what customs are appropriate and then to act accordingly.

Space. This concept is very similar to physical contact. It is that space (or moment) before physical contact. Consequently, it is easy to understand that formal people like more space between them and the person with whom they are communicating. If you stand or sit too close to a formal person, he will back away—without even knowing it, thus telling you where their comfort level is. When you encroach on a formal person's space he or she will loose eye contact and become nervous until they can distance themselves from you.

Formal people need space. They are more comfortable in large offices with big desks separating them from other people. A formal person might invite you to sit in a large chair on the other side of his/her desk. If you were an informal person in that situation, you would be uncomfortable. Your reaction would tend to be emotional; that is, you might become angry, hostile and judgmental. You would try not to show it, but it would be there. Conversely, informal people like to sit casually on sofas and be closer to the other person(s).

Formal people actually demand space. If you violate their space you create a distance in the relationship—a discomfort.

Posture. Formal people stand straight. They hold their shoulders back and keep their heads high. Informal people slouch. They like to scoot down into a chair, rest a leg up on a step. With a formal customer it would be reckless to exhibit a loose posture . . . and vice versa.

Gestures. These demonstrative actions are very closely related to posture. Formal people put their hands on their hips or fold their arms on their chests. They gesture in small, choppy movements. Formal people prefer to use their fingers rather than their arms. Informal people put their hands in their pockets and gesture in wide movements (called pinwheeling). They use their hands as combs and body scratchers!

Again, the reaction of a formal person to excessive gestures of an informal person would be non-emotional, distancing, backing away, becoming more rigid. They would distance themselves, backing away, becoming more rigid. Informal people would react to non-movement emotionally, shaking their heads and becoming outwardly judgmental.

This category of characteristics is heavily guided by international customs. For those readers who interact with business associates from varying cultures, a few rules or cautions might be in order: In the U.S. we have a custom of signalling that everything is great. Sometimes we give the "O.K." sign with thumb and forefinger making a circle with the other fingers fanned out. In Brazil, that sign will get you in a lot of trouble! In France and the French-speaking parts of Switzerland it means "worthless." In Japan it is the sign for money. And the American thumbs up sign will definitely get you in trouble in West Africa or Australia; as will the V for victory sign.

Clothes Style. From a sales point of view, this is a very important characteristic, clearly signaling the sales personality as well as the marketplace. You must meet the dress expectations of your potential customers.

This is especially true in the formal financial and professional services market. Formal clothes should be neutral and seen to exhibit high levels of authority; dark suits, neutral grays—for both men and women.

As materialistic as this characteristic is, it is highly important to this market. Physical professionalism (like it or not) is one of the key ingredients to success in this market as a sales or business development person. Formality here talks of stability and trustworthiness.

Music

Rate. This refers to the speed at which someone talks. I have found in different languages that speed of delivery is indicative of both formal and informal—depending on the language. For example, in English, formal people tend to speak faster than informal people. However, in Spanish, informal people speak faster than formal people. It is a cultural thing. Japanese businessmen I know well tell me there is a fast, almost slurred informal Japanese.

From a sales point of view, this characteristic seems to mean that formal speed of speech delivery should be deliberate and controlled. In English it means faster, rather than slower. The key words here may be deliberate and purposeful.

Volume. Formal people tend to speak louder than informal people. That tendency comes from the authoritative characteristics of parentlike behavior. It is not shouting; it is just louder. It seems to be part of the "deliberateness" referred to in the rate discussion above. In formal conversation there is little variation in tone. Conversations are non-emotional (adultlike). As you listen to a discussion around a board-room table, you will be aware of the even tonality of the conversation.

Lyrics

Language Selection. Formal people seem to speak in a language all their own. Since they tend to be highly focused, they almost create words that others can't easily understand—almost a jargon. This is especially true in business and highly exemplified in the financial/fiduciary industry. Words like liquidity, return on investment, yield—highly descriptive words, many of which have been shortened to fit the formal nature of a business conversation.

Informal language selection is made up of slang and words with a broad interpretation. Many emotional words are informal.

Topics. Formal people like to talk about accomplishments: the end result, performance, the bottom line. Informal people prefer to talk about "the journey"; how they got to the end result. They are comfortable with conversations about sharing and belonging. Informal people are quick to want to confide and be confided in.

Organization. This characteristic is one of the most important because it materially affects the quality of communication. It is also important because it is a learnable skill. Organization has to do with *how people prioritize information within the context of a question.* Formal people tend to answer questions in a direct (sometimes painful) way. Informal people answer questions more indirectly—even passively. This is known as the concept of Primacy versus Recency. If someone asks a question and it is answered in a straightforward, direct manner, the person answering the question is said to be speaking in Primacy. Conversely, if the question were answered in a roundabout—even evasive—way, the person answering the question is said to be speaking in Recency.

Figure 3.4 clarifies this concept.

The top triangle illustrates Primacy. The main point of the message (the answer to the question) is stated in immediate response to the question. The bottom triangle illustrates Recency. The main point of the message (the answer to the question) is stated after supporting data have been presented.

The following example should demonstrate this concept: Someone asks me if I like their new car. If I answer in Primacy I

Figure 3.4

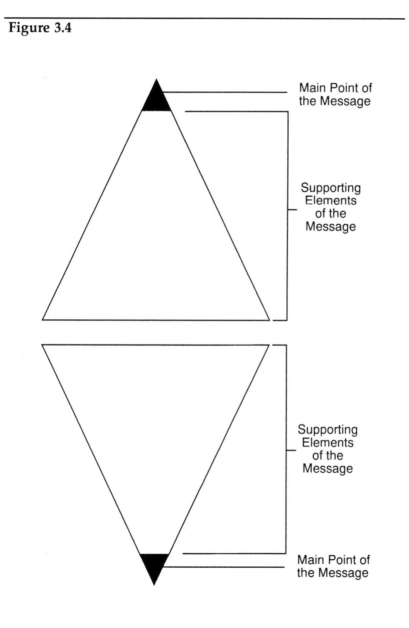

Main Point of
the Message

Supporting
Elements
of the
Message

Supporting
Elements
of the
Message

Main Point of
the Message

would say, "Yes. I like your new car because I like Buicks with four doors that are blue."

If I were to answer that question in Recency I would say, "Well, I don't know whether you know this or not but blue just happens to be my favorite color, and with my two children, and traveling the way we do, I would definitely need (and prefer) a four-door car, especially a car as nice as that Buick. Yes, I like your car.

PRIMACY	RECENCY
Yes	Blue is my favorite color
I like Buicks	I definitely prefer four doors
I like four doors	Buicks are nice
I like blue	Yes

Formal people are more deliberate and to the point. They speak in Primacy. Informal people speak in Recency. The extremes, only, have been presented to illustrate the concept. Sometimes total Primacy is cruel and unnecessary. Sometimes total Recency is evasive and unnecessary. The extremes are harmful. A thorough understanding of this concept can help develop a sensitivity to the other person, enhancing the communication.

From a sales perspective, people in Recency will have difficulty asking for the order. They are very comfortable cultivating a relationship with the client, and in the financial and fiduciary services market that skill of cultivation is highly important. A salesperson who is Primacy will tend to push too hard, not worrying about making the client comfortable and concentrating more on closing.

Often, however, a Recency salesperson will be too soft and never ask for the order, feeling that the close of the sale was implied and he or she shouldn't have to ask. It is the area in the middle between High Recency and High Primacy that is important, but having a knowledge of this concept allows for a great deal of self-examination as well as the analysis and examination of customers.

The chart below summarizes our ten characteristics.

Understanding the theory of communications is only worthwhile if you can internalize that information. The preceding chart presents guidelines for change.

If, for example, you decide that you are a very informal person and you realize that most of your customers are formal, then you must change your behavior and become more formal. So, how do you do that?

You look at the ten characteristics in the chart and rate yourself according to our numbering system. For example, my personal range of numbered characteristics is as follows:

Physical Contact	Space Limitations	Posture	Gestures	Clothes Styles	Rate	Volume	Language Selection	Organization	Topics
5	6	8	8	6	4	3	6	3	5

Overall, one might think I was informal. I have been rated as a six. That six is made up of ten characteristics and, as you can see, I have some very formal aspects to my behavior. I exhibit Primacy at an almost uncomfortable level. I talk very loud (so my wife says) and I talk quickly.

Most formal people are not highly formal in all ten characteristics. Some formal people exhibit strong informal tendencies.

A CEO might be greatly into Primacy and speak only of end-results and bottom-lines. But he might also sit at a board meeting with his tie loosened and top shirt button undone, gesturing vehemently. This mixture of signals might be confusing to the untrained observer of communications styles, but the more experienced person will recognize that an overall assessment of behavior mixes both the informal and formal rather liberally.

If a sales person is going to get along with his customer, he must align his personality with the customer. An informal salesperson interacting with a formal customer will generally result in no sale.

So good salespeople learn how to change, how to align their behaviors more closely with those of their customers. They can do that by examining these ten characteristics thoroughly and deciding which are easier for them to change.

(See Continuum Activity and Case Study in Chapter 13.)

SUMMARY

1. The formal/informal continuum simplifies transactional analysis and makes its easily applicable to sales situations. You can use the continuum (it sounds much more formidable than it is) to rate your personality and to match it better with your customers' personalities according to degrees of formality.

2. When we communicate, there is a natural tendency to align ourselves to someone else's personality in terms of space, pitch, words, touch and body language.

3. The key to effective communication is changing your personality style to more closely align with the person(s) with whom you are dealing, thereby raising the customer's comfort level.

Chapter FOUR

EFFECTIVE SELLING IS LEARNING HOW TO ASK QUESTIONS THAT PEOPLE WANT TO ANSWER

In the previous chapter we learned that success in sales comes from the salesperson more closely aligning his behavior with that of his customer . . . on the basis of formal and informal behavior and the ten characteristics that define those behaviors.

To analyze the customer's personality style (behavior) you must create an environment in which the customer talks. That requires learning how to ask questions the customer wants to answer. That skill is essential to effective communication—even outside of sales.

The person who has learned to ask questions that people want to answer is the person people want to talk to.

The study of sales techniques has become increasingly scholarly—almost as if those who write and teach sales techniques were defensive about the basic simplicity of their subjects. Many people feel that for a learning process to be accepted it must be complex and described by using words ringing of "knowledge and higher learning."

Questioning and listening should be easy. They don't need complex thoughts to explain them, only logic and order. Let me try.

If someone asks me about my children, I will spend a lot of time talking . . . because I want to. I like to talk about my children. And the person who was listening the best will be the person I will remember as the nicest; and the one with whom I felt most comfortable. The person who nodded and smiled and added little things like, " . . . and then what'd you say, Dwight?" That person, I really like. I might refer to him or her as a great conversationalist. And what a conversation it is; I do all the talking and he or she does all the listening.

A lot of the subject matter in this chapter will deal with personal conversations because personal conversations are sales conversations. People buy products from people with whom they feel comfortable. That means you have to find the communicative ground (or platform) that creates the comfort. It certainly isn't money market accounts or retirement programs!

Sadly, in our business we start talking about the product too soon. It goes like this:

Bank Salesperson: "Good Morning. May I help you?"

Customer: "Yes. I'd like some information on your checking accounts.

Bank Salesperson: "Certainly. We have three different checking accounts. Our basic checking account pays no interest but you pay few fees. Our Money Savers Checking pays 5 percent interest as long as you keep $750 in your ac-

count. And our Universal Checking account pays money market rates on the un-
used balance in your account . . . as long as
that balance exceeds $3,000 each month.
Which one would you like?"

That interchange does not create any rapport between the
salesperson and the customer. It is just one person talking at
another. The customer asked a question and the banker answered it.

Let's even assume that the customer said, "I'll take the Universal. Here's a certified check for five thousand dollars."

The bank sales person then replies, "Thank you, Mr. Jones.
Have a nice day!"

Then that banker turns to another banker and says, "Wow!
I just sold a Universal Checking Account for five thousand dollars!"

A sales-oriented banker may chuckle at that situation, but
it might hurt a little, too. It might, because the situation is all too
familiar. The customer leaves with the product he asked for and
the only thing about that customer that the banker knows is his
name. Many bankers rationalize that situation by saying, "if he
wants another product, he'll ask for it."

That rationale assumes that the customer knows more
about the bank's products and services than the banker. You
should be the authority on banking products. If you are, you
will be able to listen to a casual conversation and translate those
personal needs and wants into financial services. That's where
the relationship banker shines.

The first thing to think about is *don't rush for the product*.
That requires a sensitivity on your part, since many times customers are in a hurry. Other times (probably more often than

you think) customers would enjoy relaxing, slowing down, and feeling comfortable.

Cultivating that opportunity requires you to learn how to make your customers feel comfortable. That means asking questions that people want to answer.

Learning to ask questions that people want to answer requires a high degree of concentration. The questioning process means that you will be doing three things almost simultaneously: asking a question, listening to the answer, and planning a logical next question.

The first part is easy. The listening phase requires that you search your memory banks for relevant material and then bring it to your conscious mind where you "update" and articulate it.

Being a good listener is difficult. It doesn't mean just sitting and nodding. Anyone can do that. To be a good listener you must first ask a question that will enable the customer to listen, then you listen and concentrate, because you want to make sure the person you are talking to is comfortable. A good listener must actually believe that they are interested in what the other person is saying. If not, their opportunistic behavior will eventually become visible to the other person.

If you want to be a good listener then you have to convince yourself that you really want to learn something about the person with whom you are talking. You must feel inside that the person has some information that will make you grow—that will make you a better person by knowing it.

A good listener knows how to concentrate. A good listener has a positive approach to human behavior. A good listener has a disciplined mind.

A good listener can become a bad talker very easily. The beginning of that transition from good listener to bad talker might sound like this:

"That's interesting. I've always done it this way. First we . . ."

"Yeah, my children did that, too. Little Janey started out in . . ."

"Well, my business is a little different. We try to maintain a close . . ."

"That's a great story. It reminds me of something that happened to me . . ."

Avoid comparing what the customer says to a personal story of your own. If you get into a conversation where both parties are swapping stories, eventually that kind of one-upmanship gets boring and, worse, annoying.

Concentrate on the person you are talking to and what he or she is saying. Believe that what they are saying is of the utmost importance. You must listen and understand in order to be a good "asker of questions."

The Three Stages of Questioning

Assume that someone asks you, "What do you like most about your job?"

You answer quickly and with little thought, "The people."

Then that person says, seriously, and with a concerned expression, "What else?"

Your eyes slide upwards to the ceiling. You ponder briefly. Then you say, "Oh. Gosh. Lots of things. The challenge. Yeah that's important, too."

And, motioning encouragingly with his hand, he says, "Go ahead . . . "

Now you're wondering why he is so interested. Some self-talk is going on in your head. You get nervous and fidgety. Depending on how well you know each other, you might notice a little stiffening around your neck or perspiration on your upper lip. And then you might laugh. "What is this, a congressional hearing?"

That example illustrates the three stages of questioning.

The mind perceives questioning on a time line of discomfort that reflects an individual's propensity towards becoming "stressed." That time line is shown in Figure 4.1.

In the previous dialogue you were being asked about your job. Lots of people have asked that question. You know the answer. You don't have to think about it. That is called Chatter; the first stage of questioning/response. We do it all the time:

A.	"How are you today?"
	"Fine. How about yourself?"
B.	"So. How's the family?"
	"Just fine. Thanks for asking. "
C.	"May I help you?"
	"Yes. I'd like a checking account. "

Figure 4.1

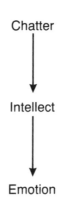

Chatter

Intellect

Emotion

Chatter is that part of questioning that we do without thinking. Chatter questions could fill a book of trivia. Everyone knows them. They are subconscious.

After you initially answered that question, you were encouraged to elaborate. That was when your mind had to start thinking. From a conscious/subconscious point of view, Chatter requires only subconscious functioning. The next step, *Intellect*, requires some conscious processing of thought. Intellect is healthy. Humans like to use their mind because it exercises their individuality—puts them apart from other people; makes them special. Everyone likes to be special. Carrying on a conversation at an Intellect level is the ultimate in asking questions that people want to answer.

Then you were made to feel more uncomfortable by sliding into the third level of questioning/response, called Emotion. This level manifests itself as nervousness, the obvious indications of wanting to leave, quickness of breath, tenseness, slight perspiration, rapid eye movement, and fidgeting. Hard-selling pushes the customer into Emotion fairly quickly. Soft-selling (if it is done properly) never gets into Emotion.

Figure 4.2 shows three types of conversations and the level of intensity from a Chatter/Intellect/Emotion point of view.

Questioning Intensity Curves

Curve 1 illustrates a strong, abrupt line of questioning. It's like when the police pick you up. They get you in that little room with the one bare light bulb and the first question they ask is, "Where were you on the night of May 17 when Dexter was murdered?"

From a sales point of view, curve 1 would sound like this:

Figure 4.2

Questioning Intensity Curves

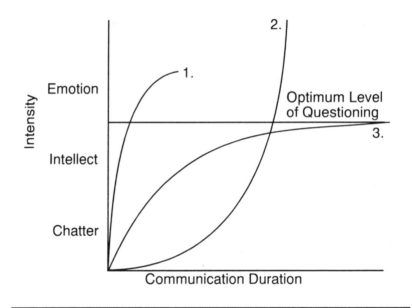

A customer approaches a salesperson.

"Good morning. I'm Todd Jones," the polite salesman begins.

"Good morning," says the customer. "I'm Mrs. Fogarty. "

"Ok, Mrs. Fogarty," the salesman replies. "Are you here to buy or just shopping?"

Did you feel it? Could you feel how quickly our salesperson went into Emotion?

Curve 2 represents a conversation that evolves into Emotion. It starts out fine and the Intellect level of questioning is used. It's just that the person asking the questions goes too far.

We do that a lot in banking when we are pushed to sell. The situation might work something like this:

A customer approaches the desk of a bank salesperson. It's Tuesday and the salesperson finds himself with some extra time. He just met with the branch administrator who notified the salesperson that if he didn't start finding out his customer's financial needs, he was never going to learn how to sell. The salesperson has decided that this is the time to try it.

"Good morning," he says, standing up from his chair. "May I help you?"

The customer, a fairly formal gentleman in his mid to late 40s, stands on the other side of my desk. "Yes. I need some information on your college loans. "

Ah, hah, the salesperson thinks. I know this stuff. "I'm Dave Knight," he says, holding out his hand. "I can help you with that. "

The customer shakes Dave's hand. "Bart Gustafson."

"Sit down, Mr. Gustafson." They sit. Dave feels very confident. He has done everything he is supposed to do.

"How many children do you have in college, Mr. Gustafson?"

"Two at present. A third next semester."

"Oh boy," Dave sympathizes. "That's a real drain on your pocketbook."

"It sure is."

"Well, Mr. Gustafson. A lot of the college loans depend on the parents' true financial needs. How much money do you make each year?"

The customer frowns and glances from side to side. Dave can't seem to understand why his customer is so hesitant. All I'm trying to do is determine his financial needs as the Branch Administrator told me, he thinks to himself.

Now Mr. Gustafson is saying something about he'd have to check his average salary and he'd get back to Dave. Now he's standing up and thanking Dave for his time.

Where was the point at which Dave went into Emotion with Mr. Gustafson? It was when he said, "How much money do you make?" That was the instant that his customer ceased to feel comfortable with him. Dave pushed too hard.

Go back over that conversation and draw a square around the Chatter part. Then circle the Emotion.

Curve 3 is the ideal situation. A conversation where the level of intensity never gets into emotion. A conversation guided by a sensitive salesperson. Like this:

The banker notices a woman in her thirties approaching his desk in the lobby of the branch. She is wearing a skirt and blouse. Heels. Looks fairly professional but the banker isn't able to determine whether she is employed as a business person or if she might be a homemaker. He stands up to greet the customer.

"Good morning. I'm Marc Miller. Can I help you?"

"Yes, Mr. Miller. We're moving into town and I'm looking at banks. May I?" She indicates that she would like to sit down.

"Certainly," Marc says as they both take seats. "Is this a job change that brings you here?"

"Actually it is."

"New job for you? Or you and your spouse."

"Both of us. We finally closed on purchasing the area distributorship for Mercer's Beer."

"So you and your husband are in business together."

"Yes," she answers smiling. "Everyone always looks at us like we're freaks or something when they find out we work together."

"I understand it's hard working with your spouse. I can't imagine working with mine. Do you find a conflict with your children?"

She leans back in her chair, slightly. "In the beginning when they were younger it was tough."

"How many do you have?"

"Three: 20, 18 and 17."

"So the oldest is in college?"

"Actually my two oldest are in college."

"Is it going to be a difficult transition for your 17-year-old?"

"Yes. We've spent a lot of time discussing that with her. I think she's ready. She understands our move is something her father and I have to do when it's available. And now is the time."

"I can understand that. Probably difficult to find a distributorship for sale in an area where you want to live."

"Especially your home town."

"No kidding. So you're from around here?"

"Yes. My husband and I both grew up here. Our families are from here."

"Well, I'll bet you're really excited to move back home. I'm sorry, I didn't get your name."

"It's Peggy Luther."

"Can you tell me about the kinds of banking services you had . . . where was that?"

"Cleveland. You know, the usual checking and savings."

The salesperson in the above situation has learned a lot of important information relative to selling financial services. At the same time he has put Mrs. Luther at ease and begun to define a comfort level between them. Marc is asking questions that Mrs. Luther wants to answer. He is being careful not to probe too much, otherwise she will become uneasy and distrustful. It's a thin line that salespeople walk. If you are honestly interested in your customer you will rarely go into Emotion. When you are probing for the sake of a sale, you will invariably "turn off" your customer. It's all in your attitude.

What do we know?

1.　Her name is Peggy Luther

2.　She is married

3.　She has three children

4.　Two are in college

5.　She and her husband are in business for themselves (Mercer Beer)

6.　They are natives of our area

7.　They moved here from Cleveland.

So carrying on a sales conversation means that you will have to concentrate. It means that you must develop a certain "respect for the human race." If you don't like people, you won't sell very well.

But the salesperson has done a lot more than "chat" with Mrs. Luther. Through that fairly innocuous conversation he has learned a good deal about her financial needs. They're probably a savvy couple from a financial point of view. Probably a bit financially-strained since they just bought a distributorship. There's a chance that the salesperson might get some of their "commercial" business. They might have some need for business loans and since it's a beer distributorship, they probably will have some inventory . . . to put against those loans. They might not have made provisions for retirement . . . unless it was with their previous employer.

This all ties into what we learned in regard to answering a question with a question. In order to keep a conversation going, the salesperson must be in charge of the communication. That means that he or she should be asking the questions. In a bank, that can sometimes be difficult since the customer historically approaches the banker and asks for a service. The beginning of the sales communication is extremely important.

Open Probes and Closed Probes

Asking questions is the key to selling and Ask Selling constantly qualifies your customer, i.e., "So, Mr. Wilson, you say that keeping $500 in your account at all times is not difficult?" That versus, "How about a checking account with a $500 minimum balance?" Asking the right questions requires the development of two important behavioral skills: sensitivity and discipline . . . the ability to "sense" when you are going too far and the discipline to stay in charge of the sales communication by asking questions that people want to answer.

With that in mind, let's break down a communication into its elements. A two-way communication is a questioning process. There are two kinds of questions. One kind of question is so direct that people can answer it with few words . . . one or two. That kind of question we will call a *Direct Question*. The other kind of question requires some thought. And the answer is extended. That kind of question is called an *Open-Ended Question*. A Direct Question when used effectively is classified as *Chatter*. An Open-Ended Question when used effectively is classified as *Intellect*. When not used effectively they can both develop into *Emotion*.

If you walk over to a stranger at a party and begin a conversation, you start with Direct Questions. In the beginning, they are harmless, but you can go too far. The following scenario should illustrate this dilemma.

Read it carefully and put yourself in the personality of Fran (either Francis or Frances). When you feel that the conversation is becoming awkward or "forced" draw a line under that question. In your mind that will be when the conversation evolved into Emotion.

Dwight:	Hi. I don't believe we've met. I'm Dwight.
Fran:	Hi Dwight. Glad to know you. Fran Hartly.
Dwight:	I haven't seen you around here before. Are you new here?
Fran:	As a matter of fact I am.
Dwight:	Oh? Where are you from?
Fran:	Aiken, South Carolina.
Dwight:	No kidding. I drove through there once about 15 years ago. What'd you do in Aiken?
Fran:	Sold pre-cast concrete.
Dwight:	Is that what you're doing up here?
Fran:	No. I changed jobs but I'm still in sales.
Dwight:	What are you selling now?
Fran:	Plumbing supplies.

Dwight:	Is this door to door or to stores?
Fran:	Stores. You know—hardware and lumber stores.
Dwight:	Oh, yeah. Is this a big opportunity for you?
Fran:	I sure hope so. I could use the money.
Dwight:	You live nearby?
Fran:	Yeah. The Eagle Cliff Apartment project.
Dwight:	You like it up there?
Fran:	They're nice but they sure are expensive.
Dwight:	That's what I heard. Did you look at other places?
Fran:	Some. Not a lot, though.
Dwight:	Nothing you liked, huh?
Fran:	Nah.
Dwight:	I'll bet you like that view, uh?
Fran:	Really nice.
Dwight:	That's what I hear. Can even see across the harbor.
Fran:	On a clear day.
Dwight:	Yeah.

That was painful! That conversation went from *Chatter* to *Emotion*. *Intellect* never entered into it at all. Where *you* experienced the sensation of *Emotion* might be different than someone else. There were no Open-Ended Questions asked. Eventually the repetitive Direct Questions became uncomfortable, and that is where you might have drawn your line. We all have different levels of sensitivity to those kinds of feelings. As I read through the dialogue, I felt uncomfortable at 9. That was the point where I felt we needed an Open-Ended Question.

Open-Ended Questions keep the communication going without that awkwardness that comes from suddenly realizing you have slipped into *Emotion*. Open-Ended Questions ask people to *explain*. They usually start out with phrases like:

Tell me . . .
How do you feel about . . .
Explain . . .
Elaborate . . .
What kind of . . .
I don't understand how . . .

In the above situation between Dwight and Fran I could have put in an Open-Ended Question at 5. Here's what I might have said:

Dwight: Pre-cast concrete. I've heard that word a number of times. Tell me what it is.

Or at 6 I could have said:

Dwight: What kind of plumbing supplies do you sell?

Asking the right kind of Open-Ended Question requires concentration. You must pay careful attention to where the conversation is going so you can spot those opportunities to ask the Open-Ended Question.

From a sales point of view, the Open-Ended Question is very important, the chance to clarify the customer's needs. When your customer starts talking, elaborating on a certain topic without being grilled by you, the quality of the information that you are receiving is at an all time high. In a sales situation, the Open-Ended Question will allow you to take notes and to analytically begin guiding the conversation.

Asking questions isn't always "cut and dry." You won't always come up with a good Open-Ended Question. Many times you will attempt to ask an Open-Ended Question and it will be answered in one or two words. That is called a *Trial Open-Ended Question*. The process of getting the customer to articulate is more difficult than you originally thought. So one goes through a process called *Re-Grouping*.

Realistically, most Open-Ended questions (in a sales situation) are answered briefly. As your customer's level of trust builds, the amount of volunteered information from your customer also builds. It is at this point that your customer begins to talk and take you into his or her confidence. Once a conversation develops momentum, one Open-Ended Question leads to another. Many times those Open-Ended Questions are not actually Open-Ended. However, the conversation, itself, has created a momentum where the customer is expanding on all questions. We call those questions that keep the conversation going, once it has been developed, *Momentum Questions*.

The following sales dialogue will illustrate the process:

General customer inquiry

> *Customer:*   I'd like some information on your loans especially for college. Do you have those?

Question/Question

> **Banker:**   Is this for your child?
>
> **Customer:**   Yes. My oldest son.

Direct Question

> **Banker:**   When does he start school?
>
> **Customer:**   In the fall . . .

Direct Question

> **Banker:**   . . . and where's he going?
>
> **Customer:**   Vanderbilt.

Open-Ended (Trial)

> **Banker:**   That's a very good school. Tell me what kind of plans you and your spouse have made in regard to college tuition?
>
> **Customer:**   Hardly any. That's why I came here.

Re-grouping

> **Banker:**   Well, there's a variety of avenues for college tuition but if you don't plan properly you can be tied down with payments forever. You mentioned this is your oldest son, so I'm guessing there are more at home.
>
> **Customer:**   We have a younger son and a younger daughter.

Open-Ended

> **Banker:**   What are their thoughts about college?

Customer: Well, I don't know about their thoughts but I do know that my wife and I would like to see all of our children go to college.

Momentum Question

Banker: You and your wife both went to college . . . and you both work now?

Customer: Yes, we did. And we are both employed full time. I work for Archer Industries and my wife is sales manager at Winger Electric.

As you can see, the line between Open-Ended and Direct is not always clearly defined. However, the process of "learning to ask questions that people want to answer" is clearly defined: i.e., *Brief exploratory questions (Direct) leading to major concepts (Open-Ended).*

The following three conversations are intended to illustrate how Open-Ended and Direct Questions interplay:

Conversation 1

Direct   "Hi John. How ya doing?"
                "Pretty good, thanks"

Direct   "Did your daughter get accepted at U Mass?"
                "She sure did"

Direct   "Bet you and Helen are pleased"
                "Yeah. We really are. "

Direct   "That makes three in college now, doesn't it?"
                "I know it!"

Open-Ended   "I'm curious—since our children aren't old enough for college—what kind of financial arrangements should we be thinking about in order to afford college?

In the above conversation, the first question was just a "throw away" . . . a greeting. The next three questions were developed to set up the Open-Ended Question. It would be hard to come out of that last question with a one-word answer.

Conversation 2

Direct	"So you're new to the area?" "Yep. I really like it around here. "
Open Ended	"I'm not that familiar with Philly. How does it differ from here?"

Conversation 2 is used to illustrate how quickly you can use an Open-Ended Question. Some people are very good at doing that without forcing Emotion. Unless you are comfortable with that style, you should allow the Open-Ended Question to evolve naturally.

Conversation 3

Direct	"How do you like your new job?" "It's gonna be great. "
Direct	"Is this a fairly good sized company?" "Not really. "
Direct	"Well . . . big enough to have a pension program?" "No. I'm not really interested in pensions at my age. "
Open-Ended	"What will you be doing in your new job?

This conversation shows how you can pursue a specific thought and your customer lets you know that he or she is not interested. Changing the topic can be a natural transition. The questioner in Conversation 3 could very well have been a bank salesperson. Instead of finishing off the series of questions after the second Direct Question, our questioner qualified the prospect for an Individual Retirement Account. Not only that but we learned how the prospect feels about retirement accounts and a little bit about what he knows about retirement accounts. Our astute questioner should log that information for future use. From a sales point of view, you should use the questioning process to determine what the perceived needs of your customer are.

Conversation 1 illustrated a normal usage of Direct to Open-Ended Questions. Conversation 2 illustrated a quick usage of the questioning pattern, i.e., one Direct to an Open-Ended. Conversation 3 was developed to illustrate a purposeful "probe" within the context of our questioning pattern.

Most sales conversations at banks start with the customer asking for a service. The salesperson replies to the customer's request with a *Question/Question* intended to change the momentum of the conversation and put the salesperson in charge. At that point the salesperson is asking the questions. That is where our knowledge of Direct Questions and Open-Ended Questions comes to light. From an overly simplistic point of view, we have unveiled a three step process: 1. Product Inquiry 2. Question/Question and 3. Personal/Financial Questioning. At this point in the sales process we should know a variety of things. Let's write them down:

1. Customer's name.

2. The product in which he is interested.

3. What they know about that product.

4. What personal and financial needs the product will satisfy.

The following Conversation Case Study will take us through the three steps but also explain the purpose of the questions and where the conversation is going.

Analyzing Body Language
It is Wednesday. 3:45. Average amount of traffic during the day. A customer approaches my desk. Male. Late 30s. He is wearing casual attire but I notice that it is nice casual attire. A cashmere sweater and button down shirt. He looks kind of "preppy." I'm assuming he is taking the day off. He looks like he should be wearing a suit and working in a stock brokerage firm. I stand up and make eye contact.

The Greeting
"Can I help you?" I say remembering to start the conversation.

The Product Inquiry
"Yeah. I read that you people have a free checking account. Is that right?"

Question/ Question
"I'm assuming that your present checking account isn't free. "
"Well, it's supposed to be but it isn't. I'm just curious to know if yours is the same way."

Direct Question *(probing to determine account opportunity)*
"Most banks offer free checking if the customer keeps a certain minimum balance. What is the balance required on your checking account?"
"It's one thousand bucks! I was really surprised. "

Direct Question *(probing for the real need)*	"So you find it difficult to keep that amount in your checking account?" "I'm not sure that's the point. I just object to paying for an account that's supposed to be free."
Empathizing with the Customer	"I can understand your feelings. I would feel the same way. It's kind of like the after Christmas White Sales where you find out that you paid the same as before they marked everything up for Christmas." "Yeah. The same feelings. Do you people do the same thing?"
Direct Question *(Trial Closing)*	"Not exactly. If you read our ad carefully you will find that we require a $500 minimum balance. Tell me, is your concern the size of the minimum balance? Because if that's the case, we're saving you $500 and you could open a checking account with us." "No. It's not really the money. It's the principle of the thing."
Direct Question *(Ask Selling Confirming)*	"Don't you think that if you have to keep $1,000 in your checking account, your bank should be paying you interest?" "Well, theoretically, yes. Why? Can you do that?"
Direct Question *(Probing for Direct Deposit and personal information)*	"Yes. With our NOW account. But the over-riding issue is whether that is the right account for you. Do you work locally?"

"Yes. I'm a Systems Analyst at Fox-croft Industries."

Open-Ended   "I've always wondered. What does a Sys-
Question   tems Analyst do, anyway?"

The last question asked confirmed the momentum in the conversation. Now the customer will explain what he does. The banker will begin probing to find out if the customer is married; the number of children; their ages; if he owns his house; what financial products do they presently have. Asking questions that people want to answer requires concentration. This process is a conscious process and requires listening skills and active thinking skills.

A well-controlled conversation comes from the interplay of Open-Ended and Direct Questions. That process might look like this:

- Direct Question
- Direct Question
- Trial Open-Ended Question
- Re-Group
- Direct Question
- Direct Question
- Open-Ended Question
- Momentum Question

Good psychotherapists know how to ask questions that people want to answer. They have perfected *Chatter, Intellect,* and *Emotion* since their success depends on establishing a continuing level of trust with their patients.

As a salesperson of financial products and services, you, too, must develop a sensitivity to each of your customers, learning how to probe effectively in order to determine their personal and financial needs. It takes practice—conscious practice and then a brief analysis of each customer communication.

SUMMARY

1. In sales conversation be careful not to start talking (or guessing) about financial services too soon.

2. Asking questions that people want to answer means you will be doing three things at once:

   a. Asking the question

   b. Listening to the answer

   c. Planning the next question

3. Be a good listener; not a bad talker.

4. In a sales conversation it is the customer who does most of the talking. The salesperson does most of the listening.

5. The three stages of questioning are:

   a. Chatter

   b. Intellect

   c. Emotion

6. Direct Questions require a one or two-word answer.

7. Open-Ended Questions require thought and an extended answer.

8. Trial Open-Ended Questions are attempts at asking an Open-Ended Question.

9. Re-Grouping is a mental process where a questioner re-thinks her order and intensity of questions.

10. Momentum Questions are those questions that keep the conversation going and occur when the customer is adjusting to the trust level that you are seeking.

11. Direct Question is any question that someone can answer in one or two words.
    "How are you?"
    "What's your name?"
    "What kind of car do you drive?"
    "Do you live nearby?"
    "Would you like a Savings Account?"
    "What's your wife's name?"

12. Open-Ended Question is any question that requires thought and a prolonged answer.
    "How do you feel about your new job?"
    "Tell me what you do. "
    "What do you like most about your car?"
    "Is it different being a grandparent?"
    "Exactly what does Trout Unlimited do?"
    "If you were me, what would you do?"

Chapter FIVE

THE SALES MODEL: AN OVERVIEW

What we have just learned about sales communication must now be structured, arranged into parts so that we know where the parts fit into the total sale.

Selling is a process. It has a beginning and an end. The beginning is the first contact with your customer and the end is the order. If you are a good salesperson, the end (the order) will be followed by another beginning since repeat sales are easier than first sales.

As you travel through the next four chapters, which have I have divided for easier comprehension and for future reference, you will increasingly appreciate the importance of the chapters you've just read on communication styles and listening techniques.

Don't be put off by Figure 5.1 which shows a sales model. I admit that, at first glance, the model can be seen as confusing, even intimidating. However, it is very simple when broken logically into its various parts. Of course, I've done that for you in the following pages.

Figure 5.1

Financial Services Sales Model

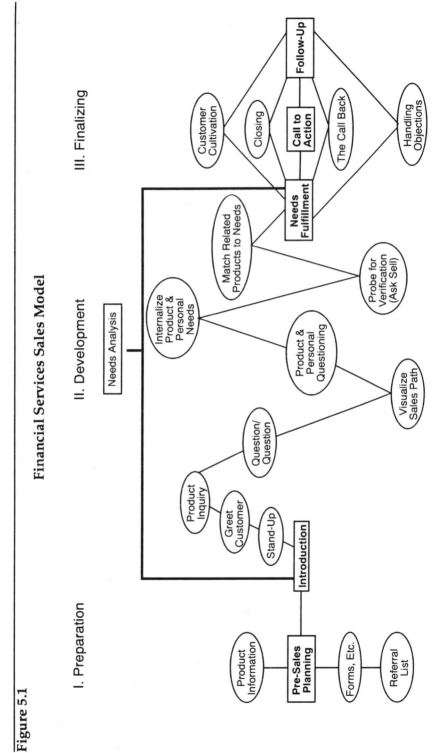

I. Preparation   II. Development   III. Finalizing

Our sales model has three very distinct stages. They are:

I. Preparation

II. Development

III. Finalizing

The model can also be presented in outline form as follows:

I. PREPARATION	II. DEVELOPMENT	III. FINALIZING
A. Pre-Sales Planning	**A. Introduction**	**A. Call to Action**
1. Product Information	1. Stand Up	1. Customer Cultivation
2. Product Forms	2. Greet Customer	2. Closing
3. Internal Referral	3. Product Inquiry	3. Handle Objections
4. Customer Data File	4. Question/Question	
	5. Visualize Sales Path	
	B. Needs Analysis	**B. Follow Up**
	1. Personal/Financial Questioning	1. The Call Back
	2. Internalize Personal Financial Needs	
	3. Probe for Verification	
	C. Needs Fulfillment	
	1. Match Related Products to Needs	

One part of the outline does not follow the model exactly. On the model, you'll notice, I have taken Needs Analysis and treated it as an overview of various elements starting with "Stand Up" and ending with "Match Related Products to Needs." I did that because all of those elements, theoretically, are an integral part of Needs Analysis. When I made Needs Analysis an overview concept, I did so to keep in mind that, even during the beginning of the interaction with the customer, you are doing a Needs Analysis. In essence, you say to yourself, "Don't lose sight of the fact that this is a Needs Analysis, not a series of mechanical steps."

From another perspective, the model will serve as a "backtracking" vehicle to identify weak spots in your selling effort. All athletes have models. Some are in their heads. Others are actually drawn out; like ours. A tennis player, for example, might have a model for his or her forehand. It might be broken down into three stages: the preparation, the swing, the follow through. Each stage would have its substages.

A serious tennis player would go back to his or her model to analyze what went wrong in a match. "Were my legs bent during the preparation stage? Did I get my racket back? Did I step into the ball? Did I concentrate on eye contact with the ball? Did I squeeze my racket firmly? Did I point at the ball with my chin? Did I think follow through; all the way through?" The expert tennis player might have an overall concept grouping as we do, under Needs Analysis. It might be "Play Your Game."

The tennis player who is serious about winning will keep going back to that model in order to keep his or her game on track. Our tennis player will refer to this model during matches; while he or she is changing sides on the court; during breaks or lying in bed at night.

If you are serious about selling to your maximum potential you'll want to study our model and outline carefully and even modify them to fit your specific environment.

Let's take the following chapters to go through the model stage by stage, element by element, to provide you with a realistic system that will create positive sales results.

Chapter SIX

THE SALES MODEL: THE PREPARATION STAGE

I. PREPARATION

    A. Pre-Sales Planning

        1.   Product Information

        2.   Product Forms

        3.   Internal Referral

        4.   Customer Data File

The first stage of our sales model, Preparation, is one that many sales people treat lightly, consequently finding themselves unable to answer important questions, remember pertinent information, or to write up an order. Basically this stage tells you how to arrange everything you need for effective selling so you will know how to get to it, when you need it. This is very important. Many times I have lost a customer because I didn't know enough about the new IRA tax implications and I didn't have a current brochure or the name of the person in the bank I could call to find out information that I needed. This stage demands that you have files, forms, brochures and referrals. It demands that you *have them*—not—simply that you know where to get them. One should never entrust any part of the sales responsibility to someone else. Here is what you will need:

Pre-Sales Planning

Product Information. Product information can take many forms:

1. Internally developed product manuals
2. Brochures
3. Competitors' rate sheets
4. Advertisements
5. Your own combination of the above.

Internally Developed Product Manuals. An internally developed product manual is the best resource for product information. It should be a three-ring binder so you can add information as well as delete outdated data. It can include a master copy of each brochure. Keep this manual at your desk. If you are a floating Customer Service Representative, keep your manual with you. It should be a personal sales resource. Your manual should be tabbed by product area. Each tab should divide structured information as described below.

The very first thing you should see when you open your manual to a particular product tab is the Sales Path. This information should actually be on the tab, itself—The Sales Path and the benefits of the product. The following illustrations show, graphically, how those first tabs should be presented.

Figure 6.1

Checking

Sales Path	Benefits
Checking ↓	Convenient. Easy to use. The monthly statements provide you with record keeping.
ATM ↓	Convenient. Much safer than carrying cash. Virtually eliminates the need for the customer standing in line.
Overdraft Protection ↓	Peace of mind. Saves money . . . a preventative banking product.
Direct Deposit	Convenient. Safe. For senior citizens, this account allows them the security of knowing their S.S. check will not be stolen or lost.

Figure 6.2

Money Market Account

Sales Path	Benefits
Money Market Account	Earns more interest than any other checking account.
↓	
ATM	Convenient. Much safer than carrying cash. Virtually eliminates the need for the customer standing in line.
↓	
Direct Deposit	Convenient. Safe. For senior citizens, this account allows them the security of knowing their S.S. check will not be stolen or lost.
↓	
Certificates of Deposit	Growth. Financial security. Peace of mind.

Figure 6.3

Certificate of Deposit

Sales Path	Benefits
Certificate of Deposit ↓	Growth. Financial Security. Peace of mind.
DDA/NOW/MMC ↓	Convenient. Less expensive. Record keeping.
ATM ↓	Convenient. Much safer than carrying cash. Virtually eliminates the need for the customer standing in line.
Direct Deposit	Forced savings are the best way to make sure you can afford that vacation or car or tuition or whatever by automatically putting a certain amount of money aside each paycheck. Record keeping advantages.

Figure 6.4

Regular Savings

Sales Path	Benefits
Regular Savings	Access to ATM. Record keeping. No fear of losing passbook.
ATM	Convenient. Much safer than carrying cash. Virtually eliminates the need for the customer standing in line.
Direct Deposit	Convenient. Safe. For senior citizens this account allows them the security of knowing their S.S. check will not be stolen or lost.
Checking	Convenient. Easy to use. The monthly statements provide you with record keeping.

Figure 6.5

Visa/Mastercard

Sales Path	Benefits
Visa/Mastercard	Convenient. Record keeping.
Equity Credit Line	Instant source of large ticket funds. Low interest loan (depending on prime or your bank's rate).
Mortgage	Investment. Buy now--pay as you go. Tax advantages.

Figure 6.6

Direct Deposit

Sales Path	Benefits
Direct Deposit	Convenient. Much safer than manual deposits. Automatic.
Checking Account	Convenient. Easy to use. The monthly statements provide you with record keeping.
ATM	Convenient. Much safer than carrying cash. Virtually eliminates the need for the customer standing in line.
Savings	Forced savings are the best way to make sure you can afford that vacation or car or tuition or whatever by automatically putting a certain amount of money aside each paycheck. Record keeping advantages.

Figure 6.7

Automatic Teller Machine

Sales Path	Benefits
ATM	Convenient. Much safer than carrying cash. Virtually eliminates the need for the customer standing in line.
Direct Deposit	Convenient. Much safer than manual deposits. Automatic.
Overdraft Protection	Peace of mind. Saves money, avoids overdraft fees.

Figure 6.8

Equity Credit Line

Sales Path	Benefits
Equity Credit Line	Instant source of large ticket funds. Low interest loan (depending on the prime or your bank's rate).
Checking	Convenient. Monthly statements provide record keeping and tax assistance.
ATM	Convenient. Much safer than carrying cash. Virtually eleminates the need for the customer standing in line.
Direct Deposit	Convenient. Safe. For the senior citizen, this account allows them the security of knowing their S.S. check will not be stolen or lost.

Figure 6.9

Mortgages

Sales Path

Benefits

Sales Path	Benefits
Mortgage	Investment. Buy now--pay as you go. Tax advantages.
Checking	Convenient. Monthly statements provide record keeping and tax assistance.
ATM	Convenient. Much safer than carrying cash. Virtually eliminates the need for the customer standing in line.
Overdraft Protection	Saves money for those customers used to paying excessive overdraft charges.

Figure 6.10

Individual Retirement Accounts

Sales Path	Benefits
IRA	Financial security. Retirement. Tax savings. Peace of mind.
Equity Credit Line	Instant source of large ticket funds. Low interest loan (depending on prime or your bank's rate).
Personal Loan	Some customers elect to borrow funds in order to purchase an IRA. Tax savings.
Visa/Mastercard	Making sure that they take the maximum contribution, this is a viable alternative for the progressive customer.

Figure 6.11

Personal Loans

Sales Path	Benefits
Personal Loans	The major benefit of a loan is what the customer is buying (or doing) with the money. Status, Financial security.
Automatic Payment	Convenient method of paying off the loan. Customer doesn't have to remember to make loan payment. Automatic.
Checking	Convenient. Easy to use. The monthly statements provides customer with record keeping.
ATM	Convenient. Much safer than carrying cash. Virtually eliminates the need for the customer standing in line.

Figure 6.12

Education Loans

Sales Path   Benefits

Sales Path	Benefits
Guaranteed Student Loan	The education at the lowest possible rate and deferred repayment.
↓	
Plus Loan	The education, on installment.
↓	
Money Line	The education collateralized by a second mortgage on their house.

Figure 6.13

Mutual Funds

Sales Path   ## Benefits

Sales Path	Benefits
Mutual Funds	Higher returns. Flexible investment vehicle. Retirement oriented.
↓	
Checking	Convenient. Inexpensive. Record keeping.
↓	
ATM	Convenient. Safer and easier than carrying cash. Virtually eliminates the need for the customer standing in line.
↓	
Direct Deposit	Convenient. Safer than manual deposit. Automatic.

Figure 6.14

Brokerage Services

Sales Path	Benefits
Brokerage Services	Diversified investments. Higher return/High risk. Flexible investments.
↓	
MMA	Convenient record keeping.
↓	
Margin Account	Ability to invest heavily, not tying up cash.

Following the divider tab (or title page for each product) should be the features of the product. There should be a page or two (depending on the product) showing rates, penalties, fees, elements and how the product works. This section might include sample forms, statements, etc. Next should be information about the benefits of the product. This page should contain sentences . . . not key words. For example, many brochures say "convenience" when what a salesperson needs to read is, "With our 565 ATM locations, having 24-hour access to your funds will be extremely convenient." The benefits page should describe the product from the customer's point of view. The next pages of the section should simply be blank so the astute sales person can jot down thoughts, key words, or product diagrams.

A major tab in your manual should be competitive information—current rates from all of your competition. In many banks that information is provided by the marketing department. I have sold at many large banks whose marketing department updates the competitive rate sheet monthly, yet when I sold in a branch no one could find one for me to use. If you keep them in your manual, you will always know where they are. If your bank does not provide you with a competitive rate sheet, you might want to use the format shown in Figure 6.15.

Brochures. Most banks have brochures explaining the product line. You should take the time to read them and underline the information on one master brochure that gives you relevant sales information. Keep the underlined master in your product information manual or a separate file. Never, never, give any sales information to a customer that you have not thoroughly read and understood. That means you will have 10 to 20 brochures at your finger tips. There are two primary reasons why: First, brochures are a major source of product information for the staff. Not quite as obvious is the fact that many brochures are written by advertising agency copywriters who have never

Figure 6. 15

Competitive Information

Competitive Financial Institution	N.O.W. Account	Savings Account	6 Mo. CD	1 Year CD	2 Year CD	5 Year CD	Mortgage	Checking	Tiered Account	Tiered Account	Tiered Account
Rate											
Minimum Balance											
Fees											
Rate											
Minimum Balance											
Fees											
Rate											
Minimum Balance											
Fees											
Rate											
Minimum Balance											
Fees											
Rate											

sold any financial services. Consequently the copy can be overly simplistic, confusing or too clever. Mostly it will be too much . . . too much copy. For years I never read a complete brochure that I picked up from a bank. When I started reading them I was shocked at the amount of unnecessary verbiage. Too many adjectives actually get in the way of explaining what the product does for the customer and describing the necessary features of the product. A good salesperson never should hand a customer a brochure and tell him or her that, "all the information can be found in this handy little brochure." That would indicate that the salesperson has not read the brochure. It also might indicate the salesperson doesn't know enough about the product to explain it. Read your bank's brochures. Be able to interpret the information for your customer. Underline important parts of the brochure for your customer. Brochures do not sell. You are supposed to be the one who sells. Brochures provide information. You should know where that information is in each brochure and during the needs analysis stage you should be able to point out that information to your customer.

Advertisements. Successful salespeople will know the image their bank wants to project to the public. That requires keeping a file on current local advertisements. Additionally, you should keep a file of competitor ads so you will be able to discuss your competition's products knowledgeably with your customers knowledgeably.

Your customers are exposed to endless ads everyday. Each bank positions itself in a certain way. That is, banks decide what kinds of customers they want. For years banks used to passively solicit all customers. But as competition got tighter, astute bankers narrowed their approach to focus on specific market segments. Some banks are looking for the upper income, young, sophisticated customer. Others are looking for the mass middle-income, blue-collar customer. Many banks target the commercial customer and use their branch network to service their commercial customers. In larger cities you will find one or two banks who cater strictly to the trust business. You can tell who your bank is trying to reach by studying your ads. Is their approach contemporary with catchy headlines? Do your television commercials use up-beat rock music and feature young, contemporary people? Does your bank talk to its market about setting aside money for the future, and use the word "nest egg" a lot? Do your ads show happy, hard working families in the back yard of their middle-income house? Whoever your bank is reaching with its ads are the customers standing in front of your desk. Of course some branches cater to certain segments of the market strictly by virtue of their location. But your bank has a master plan. It has decided who its market is, and is working on those customers.

Forms, Signature Cards. You will need everything at your fingertips. It does add to the endless clutter on your desk. I bought one of those ugly plastic organizers that hold 3 x 5 index cards (or signature cards); it can also hold piles of loan applications, IRA applications, etc. The organizer fits in my top drawer (where my customers can't see it!). The benefit of it is that my signature cards don't slide in between my loan applications, and that all of my 8 1/2 x 11 forms don't get mixed up. Many desks have built in organizers . . . mine doesn't. Know where all your forms are and constantly keep them updated so you don't run out. Nothing disturbs the momentum of a sales effort more than getting up and leaving your customer to find the right application or signature card. One form that is extremely useful in creating multiple sales is a direct deposit form. Use this form when a customer is opening a checking account and you find out he or she works for a company that has a direct deposit relationship with your bank. This form allows you to instantly direct the customer's attention to the product that you are talking about and to see the other products that could easily be offered. The sales flow using this form is very comfortable. The salesperson can talk up the benefits of opening these accounts now and creating a sense of forced savings.

In the past, direct deposit relied on the customer's getting his or her employer to institute the account. From our perspective as salespeople, we do not want to leave the responsibility of closing a sale to anyone else. Here is a sample dialogue to illustrate the use of the direct deposit form. (See Figure 6.16.)

"Mr. Wilson, you mentioned that you are working for Ace Wholesale, didn't you?"

"Yes, I did. Why?"

"Well, we have a Direct Deposit relationship with them," the sales person states, pulling a direct deposit form from her top drawer.

"What we can do, Mr. Wilson, is automatically have your paycheck deposited into your new checking account. That way you won't have to stand in those miserable lines." The salesperson points to the line in the lobby.

"I've never met anyone who likes lines."

"Well, I sure don't like them, either. So are you sure my company can do that?"

"Absolutely. All you need to do is sign here where it requests your signature." The sales person slides the form across to the customer.

"While we have this form in front of us, Mr. Wilson, it would be a good time to institute any kind of forced savings you might want. For example, you mentioned earlier that you and Mrs. Wilson like to travel during your vacations. Do you presently save for that?"

"For my vacations? I wish we did. We talk about it every year but never do."

Figure 6.16

XYZ Bank and Trust
123 Main Street, Anywhere, USA 02180

Deduct $ _____

Weekly ☐
Semi-Monthly ☐
Monthly ☐

You, as my employer, are hereby authorized and instructed to deduct the amount specified from my wages and forward said amount to XYZ Bank for credit to my account, as follows:

Amount $ _____ N.O.W. Acct. # _____

Amount $ _____ Savings Acct. # _____

Amount $ _____ IRA _____

Amount $ _____ Christmas Club _____

Amount $ _____ Other _____

TOTAL $ _____

Deductions for loan accounts will be adjusted according to payment amount.

Employee
Signature _____

S.S.# _____ Date _____

Employer _____ Payroll/Dept _____

Street _____

Town _____ Zip _____

PART 1—COMPANY
PART 2—BANK COPY

"Do you ever find that you travel to where you can afford, at the last minute?"

"That's exactly what we do. Or if I have some bonus money, we gear our vacation around the size of the bonus."

"I know exactly what you mean. My husband and I did that for years until both of us started a little vacation club where a certain amount of our paychecks was automatically put into a savings account each pay day."

"You can do that?"

"Oh yes. Very easily. For example, on this line here that says Other, let's write "vacation club" and next to it decide you might want to put aside, say, $100 per month. That means 12 months from now you will be able to travel twelve hundred dollars further." They both laugh at the situation. "You mentioned, also, how difficult it was to put your son through college. I know you've got two more going soon. We could have a certain amount put into a savings account for them, if you wanted."

"That's a good idea."

"You'll see the word "deduct" at the top of the form. Since you get raises from time to time . . . We hope . . . Definitely. Anyway, it isn't necessary to put in the amount of your paycheck there. All you need to do is write in the word remainder if you are going to have monies automatically placed in other accounts. So you put down the amount you want for your vacation club and for the other savings account . . . for college. Do you understand?"

"Oh, yes. I guess I just do that now; put the two amounts down here and here and write remainder here."

"That's correct, Mr. Wilson. And sign it right here. We will send it to Ace and when they send your paycheck to us each month we will automatically put the money into your accounts. All I need to do is get you your account numbers for you . . ."

You should check with your bank to make sure that the direct deposit form is the kind of policy they would like to institute. If the customer chooses not to open any other accounts on the form, it is advisable to request them to write in the words entire amount on the line that says Deduct. We have found there is a hesitancy on the part of many customers to divulge their earnings. At first glance this form can appear threatening if they feel they are going to have to tell you what they earn. So, in the beginning let them know that they should write in words rather than dollars. Your rationale is that, from time to time they will receive raises and each time they do, the form is no longer accurate if they list the dollar amount of their pay.

Customer Data File. Thanks to computers and CRTs at your desk, you now have access to a lot of information about your clients. With the tap of a key you can find out what accounts a customer has with your bank. You can quickly scan your CRT to find out the kinds of balances your customer keeps and, in so doing, make some preliminary judgments as to the kind of customer he or she is. Most CRT systems will allow you to do this, or almost all of this. But sometimes you need the kind of information about a customer that a computer cannot provide. Consider an experience I had. One day I am sitting at my desk and I notice an elderly woman approaching me. She is fumbling through her purse, obviously unable to find what she is looking for. I stand up to greet her and ask her if she would care to have a seat. Yes. As she is fumbling through her purse I ask her if there is anything I can do for her. It appears that she has a problem with her certificate. She can't find it. She can't remember what it looks like. Maybe Archie has it. I'm a little perplexed.

"What certificate are you looking for?" I ask politely.

"Well, I received a letter in the mail from you telling me that one of my certificates was due."

"Oh, I see. Maybe I can help. If you will be kind enough to give me your name I'll look it up in our computer. Oh, yes. Wilkenson. That's E-N." I turn to my CRT and type in W-I-L-K-E-N-S-E-N. Nothing. "Mrs. Wilkenson," I say. "Are you sure your certificate is with our bank?"

"Of course, I'm sure!" she indignantly replies. "Do you think I don't know who I do business with. You better check again. W-I-L-K-E-N-S-O-N."

"O-N. Oh, I see. My mistake." I type it the right way wanting to politely stuff her purse in her mouth.

"That's what I said, E-N. Most of the Wilkensons around here spell it with an I.

"W-I-L-K-E-N-S-O-N," I spell carefully. "I see." Lucky it's a slow day I think to myself. This could take hours. "Ahh. Here it is. You have two certificates with us, Mrs. Wilkinson. One of them will require some action on your part since it is due. Would you like to roll it over for another six months. Our one-year rate is a little bit better."

She thinks for a minute.

"Well, I didn't need to touch the principal for the last six months. I think I can do without it. Especially since the interest is better."

While I am doing the paper work on her certificate she tells me what a sad week they had—she and her husband.

"We lost Wilson. He was thirteen years old. Archie loved that dog more than anything."

"I'm so sorry to hear that, Mrs. Wilkenson. What kind of a dog was Wilson?"

"A Boston Terrier. Very bright, Wilson was. Knew a lot of tricks. Archie taught him to bring his dinner bowl to us when he was hungry."

"That's a great trick. Mrs. Wilkenson, is your address the same?"

"Why of course."

"I'm just checking," I say filling out the last of the CD.

"I think we'd like to get another."

"I'm sorry," I say. "You want another certificate?"

"No. No. Another Boston Terrier."

"I'm sorry. I'm just finishing this up and I'm concentrating on your certificate. Don't you think Wilson would be hard to replace? I do."

"You're right. Every dog we get, we'll compare to Wilson. It really wouldn't be fair to the other dogs. Would it?"

"Well, maybe not. But then again, it sounds like Mr. Wilkenson is an awful good trainer."

"That he is." Her eyes drift to the ceiling. "Yes, indeed. He is a good trainer."

We thank each other politely and she leaves. Now, it's a month later. I see this woman come into the bank. I know her, I think, as she walks up to the teller window. I watch her out of the corner of my eye desperately trying to remember her name. "Something about her dog," I mumble to myself. "Yeah. She's the lady with a dog that died . . . or was it her husband." As I wonder and try to call up the memory banks in my sub-conscious, she finishes her business and leaves. "I've got to remember," I say to myself. I get up and go over to the teller line.

"That lady that just left? What's her name?" I ask the teller who waited on her.

"Wilkenson," the teller replies. "That's E-N. " she says with a smile.

"Oh, yes. I remember. I guess she does that with everyone, uh?" I go back to my desk.

"Gotta remember that. It's Wilkenson; E-N."

Now, it's another month later. I'm sitting at my desk. A slow Tuesday. I'm counting the number of flies around my desk. I'm up to seven. Out of the corner of my eye I see this woman walk in the door. I know her. "Gaad!" I mumble to myself. "Who is that woman?" I focus in on her as she does her transaction. "It starts with a W. I know it does." I watch her some more. She finishes her transaction and starts walking past me to the door. "W," I'm still saying to myself. Then my self-talk says, "E-N." "That's it. I remember." And, as she walks by I stand up and make eye contact. She smiles politely.

"Hello, Mrs. Wilsen," I say, proud of the fact that I remembered it was spelled with an "E."

She appears startled and somewhat disgruntled. Then she looks straight ahead and huffs out the door. Then it hits me, hard, that I've called her by her dead dog's name. How do we keep that from happening? My computer doesn't help me remember her name. I can't store relevant sales information on my computer. "But," you say, "of course you can store sales information in the computer. Once you know her name, you can find out all the information on her accounts with the bank. "

But sales information is not account information. Sales information is the name of her dog. When it died. What kind of a dog it was. What her husband's name is. Sales information can also be those accounts she might have with other banks. The information in the computer is called product information—information that allows us to know more about the person is sales information. Good salespeople sell to people, not to products. Information that lets us know how customers think, where they live, their hobbies, what makes them tick. That is sales information. If you have no way of storing sales information then every time your customer leaves and returns, you are starting all over again.

Several years ago I started writing down sales information on a 3 × 5 card and filing it by customer name. I found that writing information down helps me remember it. Further, I found that filing all my cards in a little recipe box allowed me to travel with my sales information. From time to time I am required to make "external" sales calls. That means, as a salesperson, my bank requires me to call on the retailers in my town and establish some banking relationships with businesses. Whenever I get into my car I make sure I have my recipe box filled with sales information, next to me.

Let's see how good your memory is:

1. What was the lady's name?

    _____

2. What was her husband's name?

    _____

3. What was her dog's name?

    _____

4. What kind of a dog was it?

    _____

5. How old was the dog?

    _____

6. How many CDs does she have with the bank?

    _____

7. Was there any indication that there were other CDs in other banks?

    _____

Many times you will be talking to a customer and he or she will tell you they have a certificate coming due in four months at another bank. You may try hard to remember to bring that CD over to your bank, four months hence. But it is very difficult to remember each customer's financial time table. If your recipe box has monthly tabs, in addition to alphabetical tabs, you can insert a card into the month that Mr. X's CD is maturing. Each month that you check your monthly tabs you will find reminders to call certain customers. If you need to know more about those customers, you should flip to the alphabetical tabs and read your sales information. The following illustration will give you a graphic look at a very simple sales information system. You can buy recipe boxes at discount stores or office supply stores.

Figure 6.17

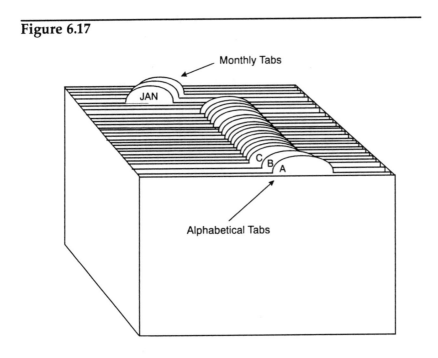

Monthly Tabs

JAN

C B A

Alphabetical Tabs

Internal Referral. Another important part of this sales information system is the development of an "internal referral list," a list of people within your bank who are sources of information on certain products. You should also list the names of people who provide back-up support to your sales effort. Today many banks have expanded their investment products and utilize experts in investment advice. With the introduction of mutual funds and discount brokerage services in retail banks, knowing the individuals who understand these services is very important. Since the field of investment products is slowly becoming more centered in many retail banks, it is especially wise to learn more about these investment vehicles and to ask the investment specialist to sit in on a customer visit with you. I keep the name of someone in the computer area if I louse up the system and no one in the branch is available to help me. Naturally I will have the name of someone in consumer lending that I work closely with; and a list of the branch telephone numbers. The most efficient use of this system is to keep 3 x 5 cards on your desk and write notes directly on a card. That way when the customer leaves, the card can be filed in the box alphabetically.

Chapter SEVEN

THE SALES MODEL: THE DEVELOPMENT STAGE

Once you have done all of your pre-sales planning, you are ready to move into the next stage, which involves making contact with your customer and beginning the process of making your customer feel comfortable around you—material we've covered before put into the sales model context. This stage of the selling process has three major parts, as follows:

II. DEVELOPMENT

A. The Introduction
  1. Stand Up
  2. Greet Customer
  3. Product Inquiry
  4. Question/Question
  5. Visualizing Sales Path

B. Needs Analysis
1. Personal/Financial Questioning
2. Internalize Personal/Financial Needs
3. Probe For Verification
C. Needs Fulfillment
1. Match Related Products to Needs

INTRODUCTION

Stand Up. The first thing a professional salesperson must do is stand up. It is very important that we greet our customers with respect. Sitting in a chair looking up at a customer is not a sign of respect. Business executives always stand up when an individual approaches their desk.

Historically, retail bankers—platform personnel—never stood up. It just wasn't done. That is because of the image of the job. Many years ago the retail banker who sat at a desk in the lobby was an order-taker. The customer asked for a product and the person at the desk gave it to him. Over time that image has changed. Now that person at the desk is a professional, knowledgeable salesperson. Part of that image is to stand up when a customer approaches your desk.

Greet Customer. Now you are standing. Your customer is approaching you. You say, "Good morning. May I help you?" A professional salesperson will shake the customer's hand as part of this process—a greeting and a handshake.

Product Inquiry. The customer will tell you what he or she is in the bank for—checking account, savings account, checkbook balancing, social security check deposit, etc. In a retail banking sales situation, the customer asks the first question.

Question/Question. As you may recall, the Question/Question keeps the momentum of the sales encounter on the side of the salesperson. The Question/Question should be the first qualifying question in confirming the financial products in your sales path.

Visualize Sales Path. At this point, the Sales Path should become a mental picture.

The Introduction part of the Development stage is a process that takes place inside your mind, preparing you for the Needs Analysis.

NEEDS ANALYSIS

The Needs Analysis is more external, meaning that the salesperson is actively asking questions and participating in a "give and take" with the customer.

Personal/Financial Questioning, Internalize Personal/Financial Needs. At this point in the sales process you should be utilizing many of the questioning skills learned previously. You should be determining your customer's personal and financial needs through a questioning process that is intended to educate rather than intimidate. A lot of the information learned through the needs analysis should be stored in your sales information box.

Probe for Verification. Probing for verification is a mental insurance policy for a salesperson. You want to make sure that you are on the right track, as far as your customer is concerned. You do this in an "affirming" way. It sounds like this:

> *Banker:* It looks like you and your husband have some sizable tuition payments coming up over the next ten years.

Customer:	I'll say.
Banker:	So far you have started a savings account. That was two years ago?
Customer:	Roughly.
Banker:	And that money is earmarked for college and nothing else.
Customer:	That's what we both agreed.
Banker:	Mrs. Thompson, you and your husband, together, make a good living.
Customer:	I know. But not good enough for four college tuitions.
Banker:	Or for two, if one of you were sick or quit. Right?
Customer:	That's right. And we've discussed that.
Banker:	You indicated to me that the equity in your house is not for college. That's for retirement, right?
Customer:	Yes. That's either our fall-back money or extra money when we retire.
Banker:	So you bought your house as an investment.
Customer:	That's why we were "house heavy" in the beginning—too much house and not enough income.
Banker:	Well, it seems to have been the right choice. You can afford it, now.
Customer:	Yes. It is more comfortable, now.

Banker: Providing college for children is a big com-
              mitment. I have some customers who have
              decided to leave that up to their children.

Customer: We talked about that but that's not the way
              we are. It is something we feel is our obli-
              gation, as parents.

In this example the banker is verifying information that has previously been alluded to or stated. The banker also wants to determine the intensity of the customer's obligation regarding tuition. These verification sessions are to ensure that your assumptions are correct, and that you haven't overlooked anything. Actually, it is a good practice to periodically verify where you are with your customer throughout the entire sales process.

NEEDS FULFILLMENT

Finally, after listening to the customer's needs and verifying your progress, it is time to put the pieces together.

Match Related Products to Needs. As you are talking with your customer, you are mentally matching products with needs. As your customer starts talking about the fact that they don't have a car and can't easily get to the bank, your mind should realize they must have an ATM card. If a customer talks about how social security isn't going to be around when he or she retires, you should realize they need to learn about IRAs, or CDs, or mutual funds, etc. There is a point in the sales process, however, when you know enough—when you are fairly certain what products and services your customer needs—when your final determination has been made. This is that point. Now, the rest of the sales process should be brief, if you have made the proper assumptions and verifications.

Chapter EIGHT

THE SALES MODEL: THE FINALIZING STAGE

III. FINALIZING

   A. Call to Action
      1. Customer Cultivation
      2. Closing
      3. Handle objections
   B. Follow Up
      1. Call back

This book has covered the final stage of selling very sparingly. Indeed, in the prior chapters, I have indicated that a good financial salesperson doesn't need to close the sale. There is, however, a lot of nurturing and and re-grouping and understanding in this broad area we call finalizing.

Call to Action

The call to action means bringing the sales visit to a close. It does not necessarily mean making a sale. It means focusing on where you and your customer are in the sales process, and what is going to be done about the issues and opportunities that have been raised. Asking for the order is not something that must be done. If you are doing a good job of determining your customer's needs, you won't have to ask for the order.

Customer Cultivation. When your customer walks out of the door; it does not mean he or she is no longer a customer. Once your customer always your customer. Providing additional information to your customers is always helpful and appreciated. Evening seminars on "investing your money" or "how to re-mortgage your home" or "planning for the future" keep contacts alive. New comers to your community might be interested in the local Welcome Wagon service or knowing where the child care services are. New businesses in your community might want to avail themselves of the local Chamber of Commerce, Rotary, etc. These memberships provide an excellent opportunity to meet other the owners of other businesses and to expand your own.

Astute bankers become involved in their communities and are members of a variety of community organizations. Because you are in the financial services business, you should become involved in many of those organizations. It is an excellent way to meet new customers. By involving yourself in community activities, you will meet many potential customers, as well as present customers. I always carry my sales information box with me and leave it on the front seat of my car. After I leave a meeting or social function I take a few minutes and write notes on who I met; where they live; where they come from; their children's names; their pets' names; where they do their banking, etc.

You should learn and store information about your customers on an on-going basis, and use that information when you meet with your customers. That process is known in the selling business as cultivation. If you have an extraordinary memory you won't have to write sales information down. If you are like most people you will. Cultivating customer relationships is a healthy process. It reinforces the reason that the customer had for coming into your bank in the first place, and strengthens your existing relationship with the customer.

The actual cultivation process is when you play back that information to your customer:

> "Hi, Connie. How was your vacation?"
> "Just great!"
> "Did you buy that dress you were looking at?"
> "I sure did."

That is cultivation.

> "Now, Mr. Jenkins. Did you ever buy that bike for your grandson?"
> "I most certainly did. How nice of you to remember."

That is cultivation.

> "Mrs. Glendale, this is Dwight Ritter calling from United Bank."
> "Yes, Mr. Ritter."
> "I just happened to notice that the local Chamber of Commerce is sponsoring a meeting on the proposal for the highway

that might run through your front yard. Did you happen to read about that?"

"No, I didn't. I am so glad you called. When is that meeting?"

That is cultivation. And cultivation is your job. It is something you should do all the time. Don't start it and then quit. It's like feeding birds; once you quit the birds will go somewhere else for food . . . somewhere they can count on.

Closing. How should a retail salesperson close a sale? I have spent a lot of time telling you that if you listen to your customers carefully and talk to them about their needs and the products and services that satisfy those needs, you won't have to ask for the order.

What you will need to do is to get your customer to agree to the new product or service. If you have been closing *incrementally* through the development stage, any apprehensions you might ordinarily feel should be dissolved. If you remember, in the needs analysis section we learned about probing for verification. That probing process is, in actuality, a form of pre-closing. Some salespeople refer to that as *incremental closing.*

When the sales situation ends up with the customer wavering and looking to you for guidance, you will have to become assertive and ask for the order. Here's how to do it:

In a tone of suggestion and guidance, indirectly making reference to the perceived level of trust that has been built, you might say, "Here's what I think we ought to do, Mr. Cromwell . . . "

Or you might say something like the following: "If you don't mind me making a suggestion, I think you might want to open up the checking account and the ATM while you are here, today. Next week I'll have all of the papers done for . . . "

"Let me just get everything in order for you. Let's see. You just sign here for your overdraft protection. This form authorizes us to automatically put $300 each month into your new savings account . . . which will require your signature here and here."

"Well, if you really feel that planning for the future is something to begin now, why don't we open this savings account and fund it until IRA time . . . "

And here is an example of how we lead up to a closing:

"Well, you indicated to me that standing in those long lines is not your favorite pastime, right?"

Chuckling, "I'll say."

"And the advantage of 24-hour access to your money is very important, especially if you're racing for the airport at six in the morning."

"Especially then."

"It sounds to me like you should get an ATM card. Can you wait for a week to get it?"

"Do I have a choice?"

"Not really. Here's our standard ATM form. Just put your signature here and . . . "

The closing process is a confirmation of the trust between the customer and the salesperson. Being sensitive to that level of trust might even allow you to refer to the account opening process as something we do. "Why don't we open this . . . " "If you're interested in higher interest perhaps we should be thinking about a longer term."

Closing depends on trust. If the trust is there, you won't have to ask or push. If the trust is not there, you will have to ask. So it is really a combination of trust and your ability to listen that makes the difference.

Making assumptions throughout the sales process that the sale has already been made is known as Implied Consent. It is subtle and should be based on needs. Here are some examples of Implied Consent, ranging from subtle to not so subtle:

"With your equity credit line, you'll be able to pay those tuition costs as they occur."

"One of the advantages of your new money market account is your ATM card."

"You'll find your overdraft protection is a source of insurance which alleviates your penalties completely."

"Now, how many weeks vacation can you afford?"

"You'll just keep your new ATM card in your billfold and when you need cash, it's there."

"Let's figure it out. The difference between X Bank's rate and your new rate here comes out to $101.50. We just made you over a hundred dollars."

When you use implied consent you must be watching your customer for affirmation; watching for a head to nod in agreement; watching that he or she is looking at you; listening to his or her agreement. Don't be afraid to make suggestions especially if they are prefaced with, "If I were in your shoes I'd . . ." or "Naturally everyone's situation is different but if I were you I'd . . . "

Retail bankers of the '90s are expected to give advice and make suggestions in the best interests of their customers. The retail banking customer of the '90s expects your advice.

Handling Objections. Objections are expressed in many ways:

"I don't know. I think I ought to talk to my husband about this."

"But First Bank offers a higher percentage."

"It's just too confusing."

"No. I'd never use that."

"Liquidity isn't an issue for us."

"But you guys are never open when I need you."

"No. We are going with your competition."

An objection is a statement of uncertainty, something on which the customer needs clarification. In a sense, it is a rebuttal. A rejection is a statement of fact, a *decision* to do something else or go to another financial institution. The terms objection and rejection are not interchangeable. Handling an objection is easier because the customer has not made up his or her mind. Rejections are made by people who are perceived to have made up their mind—perceived because in reality, making up one's mind is a constant process, and it stems from the belief that you have all of the information. But in the recesses of your mind, you may still have a lingering doubt.

"Did I make the right decision?" That question surfaces frequently with people who have made wrong decisions; and those numbers of people are huge! So rejection boils down to one person being so sure of themselves that they are willing to put their necks on the line and say no. You can believe them and say to them, "Have a nice day." Or you can assume that they must know something you don't know, and in that case you should find out what it is. The secret to handling rejections effectively is learning how to get the customer to clarify the rejection without your sounding like a bad loser.

"Whaddaya mean 'no'? How could you make such a stupid decision?"

"No" could mean "not right now." It could mean "but you didn't tell me that." No is a word that, in most cases, implies time. "It isn't timely." Or "I'll do it this way and if it doesn't work, I'll call you." Or, "It's your rates. Right now they're just not competitive."

Because we are humans, we were raised to take "no" as a personal statement implying that we did something wrong and we were bad. When you say "no" to a dog he cowers. We almost expect each other to cower, also. Therefore "no" is personal and we feel we have lost—are inadequate or whatever.

"No" is simply a state of insufficient information and until it is clarified it means "I'm not sure." If you and your customer clarify the "no" and you are both in agreement, then it has some permanence and should be respected.

"No" is not personal (in most cases) in a business situation. If you allow the personal feelings from "no" to cloud the issue, you will experience a negative emotion. That emotion is most frequently anger. The way to handle anger is the way to handle "no."

Remember: Anger, Blame, Justice, Reward . . . the cycle of anger described previously. Often the emotional shock of the word "no" defeats our ability to analyze a situation, and we are caught in a web where we are looking for revenge rather than resolution.

At all costs avoid emotion when dealing with a sales rejection. It is a communications issue involving understanding someone's real needs.

What do you do with a "no?"

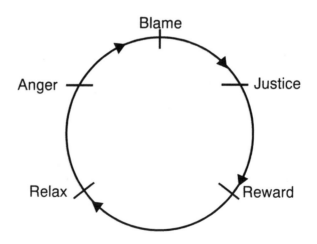

Find out what decisions prompted the "no." You might have to offer some ideas or suggestions: "Gee, I'm sorry to hear that, Mr. Collins. Was it the rate?"

In your mind, throughout the entire sales process, you have learned those points that might have caused some hesitancy on the part of your customer. You know them. Ask. Be courteous. Don't challenge the customer. Agree with his or her principles and decisions but make that agreement conditional. After a discussion you might agree with their decision and confirm the "no."

Once you have overcome a rejection then you are faced with a lingering objection. Once you have overcome the objection your customer agrees with you and understands your point of view.

Objections are either indecisions, postponements or "smoke screens" for rejections.

Here's what indecision sounds like:

"Now, Mrs. Hoppenstat, it sounds to me like you are torn between a higher CD rate and the kind of service you are used to getting from us. Is that right?"

"Well . . . I guess that is my dilemma. You know I really appreciate everything your bank does for me but money is money."

"I understand that, Mrs. Hoppenstat. So you would be happy if I could combine the two . . . higher interest and our service?"

"Of course I would, but I wouldn't expect you to bend the rules just for me."

"I wish I could but we both agree that wouldn't be right. What I can do is encourage you to purchase a one-year CD rather than the six-month CD. That way you will get a higher interest rate than our competitor and you will get us."

In handling objections, listen carefully to your customers. Understand their concerns from their point of view. Put yourself in their shoes and try to determine how they feel about a certain issue. If you can modify the product or offer a different product that satisfies the same objective then, once again, probe for verification in an "ask selling" format.

Follow Up

Too often retail bank salespeople watch their customers leave the bank without a product or service. The customers say, "I need to think about it." Some feel they need to talk to their spouse. That is a point in the sales process that is discouraging. Sometimes the salesperson might think about asking for the customer's name and calling them back but retail bankers rarely do that—call a prospective customer back.

The Call Back. The Call Back is a very important part of the selling process. More often than not, when a customer leaves in a state of indecision, we feel that customer will call back when they have made up their mind. Unfortunately, the customer may visit another bank to check out other alternatives, and that bank may sell him or her a service. The passive salesperson might have lost that sale. Statistics show us that for every 11 customers who leave your desk in a state of indecision three will return and open an account. If the bank salesperson calls the customer back, seven will return and open an account. Using effective call back disciplines will more than double the efficacy of your sales efforts with those customers who are on-the-fence.

Whenever I have tried call backs I have had a good percentage of success. In the beginning it was awkward and somewhat embarrassing. My failures came from a major flaw in my telephone sales technique, but I have since learned this important lesson: don't sell the product, sell the appointment.

Anyone who leaves your desk to ponder a choice should return to your desk to finalize his or her choice. It's "When can you come in?" not "Would you like the product?"

It is easy to tell the customer the benefits of the product over the phone. When you start, you are giving them the opportunity to turn you down over the phone. It is much easier to say "no" over the phone than in person. Additional, research has shown that people don't communicate in as much depth over the phone as they do in person.

The telephone is a separate mode of communication.

In sales we should use the phone to create a face-to-face meeting.

In retail banking sales, the phone is your way of controlling when you will meet certain customers. It will give you the opportunity to do your homework and be better prepared. Sell the appointment, not the product. The following dialogue illustrates a call back. You are sitting with your customer. She is pondering a checking "package" (Checking, ATM, Direct Deposit, Overdraft Protection). She says she wants to talk it over with her husband:

Banker:	That's a good idea, Mrs. Johnson. Especially if you both will be using the products. (We handle a customer postponement just as if it were an objection. Listen. Agree.)
Customer:	Oh, we both will.
Banker:	Why don't you let me write out the complete package for you so you can go over it

with Mr. Johnson. I'll call you back sometime next week. When is a good time to call? (Always tell the customer you will call back. Don't ask if you can call them back. Find out exactly when you can call them back.)

Customer: Oh, uh. I dunno. I get home from school around four.

Banker: Fine. I'll call you next Wednesday at 4:30 to answer any other questions you might have. I'll need your phone number. (Make sure you write the time down in front of your customer. It makes the appointment more final.

Customer: It's 663-0972.

It is a week later. Wednesday. 4:30. Here are the steps that you would go through in order to maximize your telephone sales techniques.

Banker:
(Dials the
number of the
Johnson residence): Hello. Mrs. Johnson, please.

Customer: This is she speaking.

Banker: (Step 1, Mrs. Johnson, this is Alice Brown from . . .
Name)

(Step 2, Bank)	. . . First Central Bank . . .
(Step 3, Location)	. . . on Miles Street.
Customer:	Oh, yes.
Banker: (Step 4, Permission to call)	Last week you suggested I call you . . .
(Step 5, Product reminder)	. . . in regards to the checking account package that we discussed. You indicated that you wanted to speak to your husband about it.
Customer:	Oh, yes. I remember you, Alice.
Banker: (Step 6, Ask for appointment)	AskI was wondering if you and Mr. Johnson would like to come in so we could address any concerns you might have and get the accounts in the works.

Just six steps that lead to an appointment—not a sale. In many instances the customer will decline the appointment and agree (over the phone) to open the account(s); or decide that they do not want the account(s), after all.

SUMMARY

1. Internal Bank Selling has three phases:
   a. The Preparation Stage
   b. The Development Stage
   c. The Finalizing Stage

2. The Preparation Stage involves all of the forms, signature cards, brochures, competitive ratesheets and customer files a sales oriented banker would need. In addition, this stage should include a comprehensive Product Manual which illustrates not only product information but the Sales Path for each product.

3. The Development Stage utilizes the knowledge you have learned about the human mind and Interpersonal Communications. As we have stated earlier: how to "ask questions that people want to answer."

4. The Finalizing Stage involves techniques and practices in bringing the sale to a close. It also requires us to accept objections and realize that the telephone is an absolute must for the progressive sales person.

Chapter NINE

MEASURING SALES PERFORMANCE

Most industries determine the success of their selling effort by measuring how many widgets they have sold. Sales managers look at sales figures in many ways: the total widgets sold, as well as the total of red widgets versus white widgets, the ratio of red widgets to the total, etc. Effective sales managers will spend a great deal of time analyzing various approaches to determining sales productivity. Any good salesperson should do the same. Those sales numbers are a primary self-motivating factor. Salespeople live in a world of quotas: numbers which reflect various approaches to productivity. Sales isn't the only industry that is so performance based; sports coaches, school teachers, finance managers, physical therapists, etc.—they are performance-based professions.

It is simply the language that changes from occupation to occupation. A soccer coach will analyze the number of attempted goals to actual goals. A school teacher will study grades to determine how well the students are learning. A physical therapist will measure the patients ability to straighten their knee from visit to visit. In the world of sales, our performance-based language consists of products, promotions, number of calls, proposals, presentations, rejections, acceptances. The performance aspects of our language is generally the relationship of one aspect to another.

What products can we sell more easily with this product?
How well does that new product move in territory X?

What would happen if we were to package several of those products together and instead of selling three products, we would just sell one—the new package?

Because many industries are very sales oriented, it is easy to measure sales. Historically the financial services industry has not been sales oriented. Actually financial services have avoided being sales oriented. Many financial service organizations determined that if they made money, then they sold well. It was that simplistic. Retail banks were perhaps the most guilty. If you were to ask most retail bankers how many checking accounts they sold last month, they might refer to their computer sheets and give you "total checking accounts for the month of X." But is that selling? Are the total number of checking accounts for the month of X representative of what the bank has sold?

Are the total number of funds sold by a mutual funds salesperson a true indication of how good they are at selling?

Are the total number of trades made for a client an indication of sales productivity for a broker?

Are the total number of foreign sales corporations opened by a trust company an indication of that company's success as a sales oriented company?

Perhaps not.

Customers call mutual funds on the telephone, get a prospectus and either order, or not. No one sells. It is simply order-taking.

By the time a person is ready to open a foreign sales corporation he doesn't need to be sold. He just wants to start the process. It is simply order-taking.

"Total checking accounts," as listed by most in-house computers or service bureaus, represent about 90 percent order-taking. There is a big difference between order-taking and selling! Here is a retail banking example:

A customer approaches the desk of a bank sales representative. She says, "I'd like to open a checking account."

The salesperson starts to tell her about the rates, minimum balance and number of checks.

"I'm not interested in that. I already know that," the customer interrupts. "I just want to open the account."

"Fine," the salesperson says sliding a couple of signature cards across his desk. "Will that be spousal?"

"No. Just for me. Here's a cashier's check for $1,000." The salesperson gets her an account number, some temporary checks, shakes her hand and thanks her intensely. Now, would you call that a sale?

Many seasoned retail bank salespeople call that luck!

That example was nothing more than order-taking. Yet many bankers call that selling.

If the customer would have come in for a checking account and left with a checking account, an ATM card, direct deposit, overdraft protection and a statement savings account, that would have been selling. And the final tally would look like this:

Order taking 1   (the Checking Account)

Sales 4   (ATM, direct deposit, overdraft protection, savings)

Sales expertise must be based on sales—not orders. Recently I spoke to a group of bank employees about cross-selling. After the presentation a customer service representative said, "I don't think cross-selling is so hard. Why just yesterday a customer came in and asked for a checking account so I cross-sold it to her."

We must learn how to differentiate between selling and order-taking. We should measure both. Order-taking tells us how much traffic is being generated. Sales tells us how well we are responding to that traffic.

How much do you sell? Take a guess:

1. How many people do you see each month? (This should include anybody who comes up to your desk asking for information.)

   _____

2. How many first accounts do you open each month?

   _____

3. How many cross-sales (off of those first accounts) do you sell?

   _____

Number one is your traffic count. Number two is the amount of "order-taking" that you do. Number three is the amount of selling you do.

As a salesperson, statistics are a very important part of your job. If you were selling cases of juice to supermarkets, you would know exactly how many cases you sold. Furthermore you would know how many sales calls (on the average) you had to make in order to accomplish the sale. You would know the average size of your first order by square footage of the supermarket. You would know the percentage of one juice sold to another.

The reason you would know those things is because your sales manager, in an attempt to improve your productivity, would want to examine those statistics. He or she might be asking such questions as: "Are you calling on a lot of people but not selling very many? Are you not calling on enough customers? Are you calling on customers who historically order very little? Are you spending too much time with the wrong customer?"

Valid sales veterans refer to the business of selling as "a numbers game." You should know your numbers. You should know them each week and each month. As new products are introduced by your bank, you should know how many of those new products you sold.

How to Measure Cross-Selling Efficiency within a Branch System

Every sales program should be accountable. Most are. As we have discussed, many financial institutions have sales programs whose results are not measurable. That would be like trying to set the world's record in the 100-yard dash without timing it.

You have to be able to measure performance in order to set goals. There is that old expression that says, "If you can't measure it, you can't manage it."

In the financial institutions sales business everyone seems to have a different way of measuring sales. Therefore no one understands how well they are doing in relation to everyone else.

For several years progressive banks used the *number of products per customer* as a measurement tool. So if a bank had 100,000 customers using 160,000 services within the bank, they could report that the average customer had 1.6 products, or 60 percent of the customers had a second product. For many financial institutions that ratio was interpreted to mean that someone must have sold some second products—after all, over 60 percent of the customer base had a second product. That second product was defined as a cross-sale.

Serious salespeople had problems with that approach, since they couldn't tell how many second products were actually sold. It was, in truth, the second products that represented a sales effort. Salespeople want to know how well they are doing.

Many retail banks felt they could report on how they were doing, but the figure they reported was based on the total number of customers (first accounts) and the total number of services. It was reported as a *cumulative* figure. That means that each month a salesperson's total of customers and services were added to the previous month. With cumulative statistics one wouldn't be able to see any fluctuations month by month or week by week. One could not see productivity—only an accumulation of orders.

In retail banking salespeople need to calculate a monthly *Sales Performance Ratio*. A true measure of sales performance must show instantaneous sales activity, not an accumulation of orders with one customer over the entire length of that customer's account relationship with the bank.

Several years ago a valid (though simplistic) method of measuring sales in a retail bank was developed. This method measured sales *on a monthly basis*. It measured the efficiency of selling a second product (the cross-sale) off of the first product (the order). It reported that efficiency as a percentage. Therefore, stated simply, *true sales performance should be the percentage of second products sold to first products—stated on a monthly basis.* Diagram 1 illustrates how one calculates that percentage:

Step 1.

Total First Accounts

+ Total Second Accounts (cross–sales)

= Total Accounts

Step 2.

Total Accounts ÷ Total First Accounts = Cross-Sales Ratio

Research with over 25,000 internal bank sales personnel has revealed that an average, untrained customer service representative (CSR) will cross-sell (approximately) two out of every 10 first accounts. Calculated as a ratio, that CSR would have a 1.20 ratio, i.e., a 20 percent efficiency. The average bank that has undergone sales training is capable of maintaining a ratio of 1.80 which means a cross-sale for eight out of every ten customers (80 percent). That ratio is calculated every month. So a customer who came in last month and opened one account and was sold a second account is considered a first account all over again, each month. This ratio is *not* cumulative. It should not be a *Relationship Banking ratio.* Relationship Banking is a marketing concept and cannot be used as an accurate measure of *real sales performance.*

The CSR who cross-sells every single customer every month would have a ratio of 2.00.

As an exercise in a realistic sales situation, calculate the following ratio for the customer service representative:

Activity—Calculation of a cross-sales ratio

Total new accounts opened during the month	81
Total cross-sales	11
Cross-Sales Ratio	

This method of measuring sales performance is not affected by traffic, since it is a ratio which illustrates one kind of selling (order-taking) and its relationship to another kind of selling (cross-selling). It *is* affected by the relationship between first and second accounts. And although this ratio is not 100 percent accurate as a measurement device, it is a recognized standard by which many banks measure their sales productivity.

You will meet people who will tell you they have a ratio of 3.60. In most cases a salesperson with a 3.60 ratio accumulates multiple products on a first account from the day that customer first opened that account. If you were to ask that 3.60 sales person how many times a specific customer can be listed as a first customer, they will tell you only one time. In a sales performance ratio a specific customer is listed as a first customer every time he or she walks into the bank and opens an account. That salesperson will have 30 days to create multiple sales, after which time the customer will return to "first account" status.

There are other types of sales ratios in banking, so be sure, if you are comparing sales performance with another banker, that you are comparing "apples to apples."

There are many instances when you are too busy to sell. A busy salesperson would open over 100 first accounts. In most cases, over 100 is considered too busy to sell. There are many banks in congested metropolitan areas where the *average* number of first accounts can be as high as 120 per month. Most CSRs do approximately 60 to 70 first accounts.

Here are a few "rules of thumb":

If you do 70 first accounts, you probably will "wait on" 210 customers. Three times the number of first accounts is traffic. If you are cross-selling 50 percent of those 70 first accounts, you are an average, professional retail bank sales person.

Those percentages are called the "3-to-1-to-1/2 factor," meaning the average traffic is three times the number of first accounts and half of the number of first accounts should result in cross-sales.

Branch managers find it difficult to achieve those kinds of numbers. The managers are trying to run a branch. In many cases branch managers find themselves with a 2.00 ratio. Don't be too impressed. Due to their work load they might have waited on two customers and took the time to make sure they had everything they needed. So two first accounts and two second accounts give you a 2.00.

You will also find that branches differ in the average ratio of their salespeople. For example, the salespeople at branch 1 might have a ratio of 1.18 after nine months of tracking, while those at branch 2 might have a ratio of 1.35. That doesn't necessarily mean that branch 2 is better. It probably means that branch 1 has an older customer base than branch 2. It might mean that branch 2 has more of a young, affluent market. Younger, more aggressive individuals are more likely to buy several banking services than are older individuals who find it more difficult to accept the need for many of today's financial services.

A branch with an average ratio of 1.25 might be slightly low because each salesperson there is doing more than 80 first accounts per month. A smart sales manager will suggest adding another salesperson to improve the overall productivity of the branch.

A final element of sales measurement is called *new money*. *New money* is money from another bank that a customer uses to open a new account. *Transferred money* is money that is transferred out of one of your bank's accounts and used to open another account. Banks realize more profits from *new money* than *transferred money*.

Measuring new money is fairly easy and it tends to relate your sales efforts to the bottom line more easily.

The following case study illustrates another way of looking at the cross-sales ratio and determining how much money can be tied to a ratio point.

A Case Study

ABC Bank has assets of $450 million and ten branches. Their tracking system reveals a sales performance ratio that started at 1.11 and is currently at 1.61, after a one-year sales training program for their employees.

Let's examine this ratio carefully in relation to the amount of *cross-sold new money* that the bank has brought in. We know, for example, that the bank started with a ratio of 1.11. That means that 11 percent of the first accounts were accompanied by a second account. We know that at month 12 their ratio was 1.61 or 61 percent efficiency. That 61 percent efficiency accounted for $677,000 of cross-sold (second account) new money in that 12th month. Chances are they were not tracking new money in the past. With the following calculation we can estimate how much new money their cross-sales were bringing in before the program began:

$$\frac{.11}{x} = \frac{.61}{\$\ 677,000}$$

$$x = \$\ 122,081.96 \text{ (cross-sold new money before program)}$$

By simply subtracting the first month's figures from the twelfth month's figures we can get an approximation of how much additional money we are now bringing in.

We know that the selling effort is creating $554,918.04 more of monthly cross-sold new money per month.

You should be familiar with what you sell and how you sell. Using a ratio will be very helpful in setting goals for yourself . . . and your staff.

Order-Taking to Sales Ratios in Other Financial Services Businesses

In the mutual funds industry a performance ratio would consist of the "called-in-for" fund as the first account and the money-market fund or discount brokerage or annuity as the second account. A realistic ratio can be set up using these criteria which will show sales productivity. This ratio will be different than the retail banking ratio since the sales environment is totally different.

Stockbrokers can create cross-sales ratios by simply determining the *lead product* and dividing the number of lead products into total products.

SUMMARY

1. The financial and fiduciary services industry rarely measures sales performance—only total sales.

2. An effective measurement of sales performance within a bank is calculated as follows:

Step 1.

Total First Accounts
+ Total Second Accounts (cross–sales)

= Total Accounts

Step 2.

Total Accounts ÷ Total First Accounts = Cross-Sales Ratio

3. Some "rules of thumb" for selling in a retail bank are:

a. 1.20 is average for an un-trained salesperson

b. 1.50 is average for a trained salesperson

c. 2.00 means cross-selling every customer.

Section THREE

Relationship Products/Services

Chapter TEN

THE NEWEST PARTNER/COMPETITOR IN RETAIL BANK INVESTMENT PRODUCTS

In the late '80s and early '90s, when returns on certificates of deposit dropped to record lows, mutual funds became the logical successor to the CD. Retail bankers knew very little about mutual funds. Their customers knew very little, also. As returns continued to hover in the three to four percent area, banks began looking at mutual funds as a new product they could sell since their customers were anxious to receive higher returns, and so were interested in buying.

The problem with this natural marketing process is that retail bankers forgot to fully educate their sales staff on what mutual funds are and how ones sells (or refers) them. This chapter is intended to assist the retail banker with background information and definitions of mutual funds. Later in this book the reader will learn how one sells mutual funds and how one cross-sells *off of* mutual funds, or cross-sells *to* mutual funds.

One of the major changes in the growth of the financial services industry has been due to the introduction of mutual funds. It is a new industry that grew from the traditional stock brokerage services of the past. It has been a logical expansion of a traditional service—caused by the end-user becoming increasingly aware of various investment alternatives and eventually deciding to put his or her money "in the stock market."

The Best Long-Range Investment Vehicles

As financial information became more readily available due to advancements in technology, the average investor learned that the best long-range investment was clearly the stock market. The following table shows the total return on a variety of investment alternatives.

It is quite clear that over the long run, common stocks outperform other investment vehicles. The above chart does not reflect a 26 percent increase in 1991 and a 4 percent increase in 1992. Clearly short-term volatility is often the cause for customers choosing more predictable investments.

The problem with investing in common stocks is that individuals pick stocks for a variety of reasons . . . reasons that have little to do with whether the value of the holding will increase or decrease. I am reminded of my father who picked IBM in 1959 because "it's easy to remember—only three letters." He was lucky; luckier because he bought it and forgot that he had it for ten years. I bought Sovereign Industries when I was 18 because I liked the sound of the name—Sovereign. It went broke in the early '60s.

Mutual Funds—Defined

It wasn't until the average investor was smart enough to understand the concept of "bundling many stocks, bonds or other securities into one fund" that the mutual fund industry began to take off. And that is precisely what a mutual fund is—a bundling of many stocks, bonds or securities into one fund. Many mutual funds are huge, like the Magellan Fund of Fidelity Investments. Magellan owns literally thousands of stocks and is worth over $24 billion. It dwarfs most other mutual funds since there only a few who can boast over a billion dollars in holdings.

Categories of Mutual Funds

These mutual funds are managed by people who study the equity and bond markets carefully. They buy stocks and bonds for their funds. Their choices for stocks and bonds segment each fund into a category. The following categories of stock funds reflect the investment philosophy of the fund manager:

Aggressive Growth. Seeks maximum capital gains, often in small-company stocks.

Long-Term Growth. Seeks capital gains, often in large-company stocks.

Growth and Income. Emphasizes safety and yield.

International and Global. Invests totally or primarily in non-U.S. stocks.

Sector Funds. Specializes in investing in one industry or portion of the economy, or precious-metal stocks.

Bond funds, also, are categorized according to investment philosophy:

Investment-Grade Corporate. Emphasizes safety by owning high-rated (low-risk) corporate bonds.

High-Yield Corporate. Seeks higher yield by owning higher-risk corporate bonds.

Investment-Grade Tax-Exempt. Emphasizes safety by owning low-risk municipal bonds.

High-Yield Tax-Exempt. Seeks higher yield by owning higher-risk municipal bonds.

U.S. Government. Owns Treasury securities or those of federal agencies.

Mortgage. Owns mortgage-backed securities, like Ginnie Mae issues.

International and Global. Invests at least partially in non-U.S. bonds.

Each of these funds report their success (or failure) in terms of some kind of a return number—a percentage gain (or loss). The best return number to use is called *total return*. This number is the sum of the yield plus the change in market value of the investment. It is expressed as a percentage change.

With the increase in popularity of mutual funds, those companies who provided technical support to the industry also took off. A major industry is now made up of companies who provide administration services to the over 3,000 mutual funds around the world; companies who provide full accounting services and calculate daily Net Asset Values through intricate computer hook-ups and ever-changing software.

Mutual Funds as an Industry—Today

The mutual fund business reached an all-time high in January of 1993, as U.S. investors poured $20.7 billion dollars into stock and bond funds. Of this total, $10.2 billion went into stock funds and $10.5 billion went into bond funds. The interesting thing to realize if you are marketing investment vehicles to consumers, is that the U.S. investor took $20.7 billion dollars out of other investments to put into stock and bond funds. Experts estimate that $14 billion came from retail bank CDs and approximately $6 billion from purchases and switches from other funds.

Mutual funds are still stocks, or bonds. Unlike a bank certificate of deposit which is insured by the FDIC, a customer can lose principal (capital) in mutual funds. In 1992 one of the largest and most successful funds, Twentieth Century Growth, lost money. So if an elderly person looking for better than 3 percent from CDs invested in Twentieth Century Growth in January of 1992, by January of 1993 he or she would have lost approximately 4 percent of their capital!

Because of situations like that capital loss, most funds are rated according to risk, so an investor can calculate the degree of risk. At first, the process of measuring risk sounds confusing, but with just a little concentration anyone can calculate risk. The risk-of-loss factor is the potential for losing money in a fund calculated as follows: The monthly Treasury bill return is subtracted from the fund's total return for each of the 60 months in the rating period. When a fund has not performed as well as Treasury bills, the result is negative. The sum of these negative numbers is then divided by the number of months in the period. The result is a negative number, and the greater its magnitude, the higher a shareholder's risk of loss.

The growth of the mutual fund industry is closely correlated to the fluctuations of our own stock markets; so if the S&P

is growing at a rate of 20 percent (as it did in 1991), the average mutual fund will grow similarly. Conversely, if the S&P grows at just under 7 percent, the average mutual fund will do the same. Also remember that *most mutual funds do not out-perform the S&P 500*. That is a fact. Therefore, the down-side to a slow market (where the S&P is returning 7 percent and over half of the mutual funds are under-performing the S&P 500) is that many clients with high aspirations will be very disappointed. That makes the 3 percent federally guaranteed certificate of deposit very attractive!

From a sales point of view, the consumer knowledge of mutual funds' rate sensitivity—especially as a result of the 1992 mutual fund performance—will make consumers more skeptical in the future and less likely to leave their retail bank in search of a high earning mutual fund quite so quickly. Therefore, the sale will be more difficult. Consumers will want more information. And they will want that information presented in a language they understand, because they can always go back to that safe, simple-to-understand, insured CD.

The Bond Fund as a Hedge against Interest Rates

Let's examine bond funds. Historically, we all have learned that as interest rates go down, bond returns go up. Expressed from more of a consumer perspective, if mortgage rates go down, bond rates should go up. And all other things being equal, that pretty much is the case (severe economic conditions tend to water down that theory).

Bonds, themselves, are measured according to the Lehman Brothers Government/Corporate Bond and Municipal Bond index. Figure 10.1 accurately illustrates the return.

Figure 10.1

For the following periods ending 12/31/90	Common Stocks	Long-Term Govt. Bonds	Long-Term Corporate Bonds	Intermediate-Term Govt. Bonds	U.S. Treasury Bills	Consumer Price Index
1 year	-3.2	6.2	6.8	9.7	7.8	6.1
3 years	14.1	11.2	11.2	9.7	7.5	5.1
5 years	13.1	10.8	10.4	9.3	6.8	4.1
10 years	13.9	13.7	14.1	12.5	8.5	4.5
20 years	11.2	8.7	9.0	9.1	7.7	6.3
30 years	10.2	6.2	6.8	7.3	6.5	5.1
40 years	11.6	4.9	5.5	6.1	5.4	4.3
50 years	12.0	4.5	4.9	5.2	4.4	4.8
Since 1925	10.1	4.5	5.2	5.0	3.7	3.1

Source: Ibbotson, Roger G., and Rex A. Sinquefield, *Stocks, Bonds, Bills, and Inflation* (SBBI), 1982, updated in *Stocks, Bonds, Bills and Inflation 1991 Yearbook*™, Ibbotson Associates, Inc., Chicago. All rights reserved.

Common Stocks (S&P 500)—Standard and Poor's Composite index, an unmanaged weighted index of the stock performance of 500 industrial, transportation, utility and financial companies.

Long-Term Government Bonds—Measured using a one-bond portfolio constructed each year containing a bond with approximately a twenty year maturity and a reasonably current coupon.

Long-Term Corporate Bonds—For the period 1969–1990, represented by the Salomon Brothers Long-term, High-Grade Corporate Bond Index; for the period 1946–1968, the Salomon Brothers Index was backdated using Salomon Brothers monthly yield data and a methodology similar to that used by Salomon Brothers for 1969–1990; for the period 1925–1945, the Standard and Poor's monthly High-Grade Corporate Composite yield data were used, assuming a 4 percent coupon and a twenty year maturity.

Intermediate-Term Government Bonds—Measured by a one-bond portfolio constructed each year containing a bond with approximately a five year maturity.

U.S. Treasury Bills—Measured by rolling over each month a one-bill portfolio containing, at the beginning of each month, the bill having the shortest maturity not less than one month.

Inflation—Measured by the Consumer Price Index for all Urban Consumers (CPI-U), not seasonally adjusted.

Many investors, especially those interested in security with a predictable return, will be more interested in bond funds than aggressive stock funds.

Many investors who have been actively involved in the stock and bond markets on their own are skeptical of funds. Their skepticism is based more on ignorance than skill, since the diversification benefits of funds far outweigh individual efforts—in most cases.

SUMMARY

1. In the late '80s and early '90s when returns on certificates of deposit dropped to record lows, mutual funds became the logical successors to the CD.
2. The investor has learned that the best long-range investment is clearly the U.S. stock market.
3. Mutual funds are the bundling of many stocks or bonds into one fund.
4. Mutual fund managers invest in stocks or bonds and their funds fit into categories which reflect their investment philosophy.

    Stock fund categories are:
    Aggressive Growth
    Long-Term Growth
    Growth and Income
    International and Global
    Sector Funds

    Bond fund categories are:
    Investment-Grade Corporate
    High-Yield Corporate
    Investment-Grade Tax-Exempt

High-Yield Tax-Exempt
U.S. Government
Mortgage
International and Global

5. Total return reflects the productivity of the fund by measuring growth, including all expenses.

6. The risk-of-loss factor is the potential for losing money in a fund.

7. The growth of the mutual fund industry is closely correlated to the fluctuations of our own stock and bond markets.

Chapter ELEVEN

SELLING "OFF OF" LEAD PRODUCTS IN THE RETAIL BANKING BUSINESS

From a sales point of view, retail banking is a unique business. First of all, the customers come to the salesperson. The salesperson doesn't have to pack an attaché case and go door-to-door selling checking accounts. Customers come in and generally ask for a product. The bank salesperson pulls out an order pad and writes it up. It's all very similar to waiting on tables.

Bankers sitting at desks taking orders used to be enough. Creating profits through expanded customer relationships meant that those bankers had to begin to sell. In the minds of most bankers were visions of being pushy and offensive to their customers. They didn't want to sell. But as the pressure began escalating, they started saying, "How about a checking account?" They called that selling. Under severe pressure from management, they might follow up that checking account with, "How about an ATM card?" Quite frequently that would work.

They didn't like to do it. That type of selling is called *How'bout'a Selling*.

It works from time to time because bankers are in the business of offering many products that are related to each other. Fast food businesses capitalize on that kind of situation; a customer asks for a cheeseburger and the clerk asks if they want french fries with it.

The big difference between the fast food business and the banking business is that the clerks have been *told* to offer french fries. No one told them why. It is just a rule. I visited McDonald's last summer and ordered a soft ice cream. The clerk said, "You want french fries with that?"

In the banking business many products are related to each other, but the customers don't perceive bankers as waiters or waitresses. Bankers are perceived as professionals who know ways to insure present and future financial stability. Selling financial services is a job that requires the salesperson to think— to match needs with services.

The Sales Cycle

Every selling situation can be broken down into a pattern. Some people refer to these patterns as sales cycles. Retail bank selling can also be viewed as a cycle. The sales cycle starts with the customer asking for a product. The salesperson has a basis for internalizing (or understanding) their needs. The salesperson can "probe" (or question) for clarification of those needs. Matching related products to those needs is simply a mechanical process. Finally, the banker guides his or her customer toward a close. Effective financial services salespeople don't concentrate on the close. People who concentrate on the close will generally Hard-Sell.

The key elements of our sales cycle are shown in Figure 11.1.

An important part of the retail banker's job is to take advantage of the fact that customers are coming and asking for a product. If you understand related products and services and have committed to memory the related products of those products/services that you sell most frequently, creating multiple sales from each customer becomes easy.

Identifying Your Lead Products

Retail bankers don't sell many products. That is a fact. Even though the bank offers dozens of services, the average retail

Figure 11.1

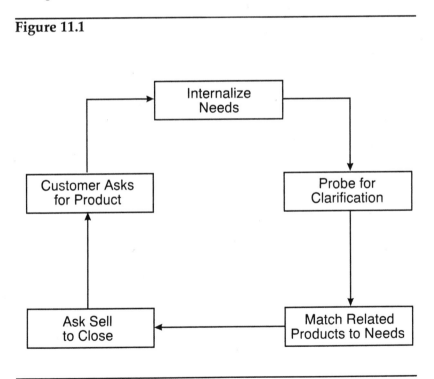

bank salesperson sells (1) Checking, (2) Savings, (3) and some CDs. In the retail banking business, these are called *lead products*.

Each of us handles a different flow of customers. Our customer profile differs widely from branch to branch. If you are in a branch with predominantly older customers (in their retirement years), you will not understand how some of your fellow employees are opening 40 percent or 50 percent checking accounts in other branches. Conversely, those employees can't understand why you are doing 50 percent CD roll-overs and 5 percent checking. In affluent areas with a younger customer base, a busy banker will open 80 percent checking.

Let's see exactly how a retail banker's business stacks up. What is the relative weight of their lead products?

If you are a retail banker, the following exercise (Figure 11.2) would be most helpful: Estimate what percentage of all the accounts you open are checking accounts and put that figure in the first box. Do the same for the boxes under "savings," "CDs," "loans" and "other." Make sure they total 100 percent.

After you have estimated the weight of your lead products, list under the "other" box what other accounts you open as first accounts.

Now you can get an overview of what you do in the area of opening accounts.

Figure 11.2

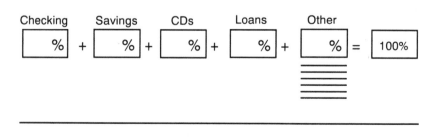

Before I started my first day as a retail bank salesperson, I was apprehensive and quite scared. I was working for a bank that offered all of the customary retail banking services—twenty or thirty of them. I was going to be barraged by angry customers asking me questions about twenty or thirty products. I studied feverishly for two weeks before nervously taking my seat at a desk. After several weeks I began wondering if my branch was different than other people's branches. Where were all of the people asking about mutual funds, Keoghs and discount brokerage, letters of credit, foreign exchange, bi-monthly mortgages? I had mastered the money market account and not one single customer asked for it. "Strange customer base," I mused.

Slowly, I began to realize that I was only selling three products. That was it! In real language, I was filling out orders for three products and selling nothing. But I wasn't trained to sell. Since I wasn't trained, all I did was react to my customers. I did what they asked for. They asked for Checking Accounts, Savings Accounts, and some CDs. Those three accounts represented 90 percent of my orders. Why in the world did I spend so much time memorizing features of products that no one asked for?

The reality of the retail banking world is simple: The bank salesperson's job is to learn how to take orders on three products (our lead products) and then sell *off of* those three—that is, cross-sell.

You should learn about the twenty to thirty products in your bank, but learn about them in the context of how they relate to people's primary financial needs.

This is true in retail banking, selling mutual funds by phone, business banking, or being an attorney or accountant. Financial and fiduciary services rely on an initial service (a lead product) off of which one sells related services.

A non-banking example:

A person contacts a law firm in order to have a will drawn up. That person establishes a relationship with the attorney. In the process of the conversation regarding the will, the topics of retirement and pension funds arise. The client is referred to the pension specialist in the firm. Later, the client calls the primary contact at the law firm to have an attorney represent him in a pending litigation because he head been pre-sold on the firm's other areas of legal expertise.

Just like financial services, the lead product opened the door, followed by cross-sales.

Law Firm Product Sales Flow: Will → pension plan → litigation.

Visualizing Lead Product Related Services

Now that we know which products are the retail banking lead products, we can anticipate what can be sold *off of* those lead products. Each product has a support product which can further customize it for a particular customer. For example, an upwardly mobile, young executive who travels frequently and writes many checks would need, as her lead product, a checking account. Further customizing that checking account would be an ATM card so she can get cash when she is on her way to the airport at six in the morning. And to make sure her paychecks get deposited, so she doesn't have to stand in line each month, we would cross-sell direct deposit to her checking account. Finally, to cover her "financial indiscretions," we would cover her with our overdraft protection. So this particular customer who comes in and asks for a checking account would leave with (1) a checking account (2) an ATM card (3) direct deposit and (4) overdraft protection.

That product mix would not apply to a nineteen-year-old college student who receives an allowance from home. Or the seventy-year-old living on her investment yields. Yet the lead product is the same. And simply by looking at the customer and asking a few brief questions, an astute banker can determine the cross-sales possibilities for each customer. Selling is a numbers business and we should pay attention to the averages; i.e., the *average* customer we wait on; the *average* product mix available to that customer.

Figure 11.3 shows a "Lead Product Sales Path." This chart shows that the average retail bank salesperson sells six products. Of these six, three (Checking, Savings and CDs) account for 90 percent of their orders.

Let's discuss these paths.

Checking to ATM to Direct Deposit to Savings to Overdraft Protection

The prime user of the checking account sales path is twenty-two to forty-years-old, married, of middle to upper income, and college-educated. The path is easy to orchestrate. The customer should be sold the ATM as part of the checking account. "It's free and standard equipment on our checking account." You won't need much more than that.

In numerous test cases throughout the U.S., I was able to sell 91 percent of my checking accounts an ATM card. If I took a lot of time and explained the fact that the customer could use the card 24 hours a day in 4 million locations—if I went into that kind of detail, I was wasting my time and the customer's. You can sell an ATM card without that. *Don't oversell.* ATMs are widely understood and widely used. Twenty years ago a bank with ATM cards was experiencing 15 to 20 percent usage. Today that figure is closer to 90 percent.

Figure 11.3

Lead Product Sales Path

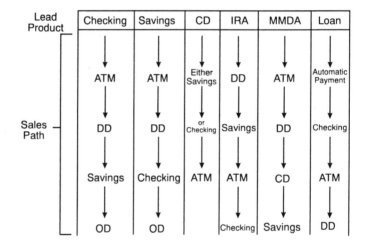

Key:
CD = Certificate of Deposit
IRA = Individual Retirement Account
MMDA = Money Market Account
ATM = Automatic Teller Machine
DD = Direct Deposit
OD = Overdraft Protection

If your lead product is a checking account, as you are providing information to your customer you are simultaneously setting the ground-work for the related products.

Once your customer appears interested in opening a checking account, you say, "Do you work locally?"

You are now probing for direct deposit. Not necessarily direct deposit in the strictest of EFT terms, but a service that automatically will put the customer's paycheck in the bank and eliminate the long lines.

My company doesn't have formal direct deposit relationships with any banks, but if any of my employees wants their check sent to *their* bank, we are happy to do that for them. So are most businesses. Many banks are providing a simple form for the customer to sign which authorizes the employer to send the employee's paycheck to the bank. A form like that will insure that your customer's paycheck is in the bank. The customer doesn't have to stand in long lines, and you have gained an element of trust from your customer by providing such a service.

A copy of the direct deposit form and an explanation of its usage can be found in Chapter Six.

Once your customer has a checking account, direct deposit, and an ATM card, you should realize that you have an active consumer, i.e., a customer who is open to convenience banking services. Overdraft protection or cash reserve could be the next logical cross-sell. Overdraft protection is a protection for the customer, who looks at it as an astute judgment on your part to suggest the service. It is one more element of the trust you are building.

Each account you sell a customer should increase the level of trust between you and that customer. Statistics show us that if a customer has one service with your bank, there is a 30 percent chance of keeping him or her. If your customer has two services, your chances are 50 percent. If your customer has three services, your chances are 70 percent. And with four, you are at 90 percent. Eventually, you will develop the kind of relationship where all you need to say is, "You know what you need, Dan/Connie . . . "

At this point in our Checking Account Sales Path, we might let our customer go because suggesting anything else could begin to make the customer feel uneasy. However, we are not finished with that customer. As we gain a little more respect and trust from him or her, we know that we can start talking about a "forced savings" program. But we might hold that for another visit.

Savings to ATM to Direct Deposit to Checking to Overdraft Protection

This is an interesting path. It's interesting because there are actually two savings accounts: statement and passbook. Statement savings is a natural product to sell off of. Passbook savings is almost a dead-end account as far as cross-sales go. Now, I'm sure that there is a bank employee somewhere who has developed an effective path for passbook savings. I would certainly like to know about it.

Each of the two savings accounts has a different prime customer. The passbook savings customer is generally an older individual who has had a passbook account for many years and therefore has developed a dependency on the book. It is difficult to get a passbook-dependent customer to change to a statement account. Usually, if a customer is in your bank asking for a passbook account, it is because they just moved in locally, or that the bank the customer was with tried to get them to accept a statement account. The over-sixty individuals who want a passbook account will settle for nothing else. An ATM does not apply. Sometimes they will need and accept a checking account. You might get some of their CD business, but in order to sell those customers you will need to learn more about concepts in interpersonal communications and "how to ask questions that people want to answer."

A customer asking for a statement savings account can utilize an ATM as easily as a checking account. It's sold the same way—as part of the savings account. "It's standard equipment on our savings account and it's free." You will find that most people who want to open a statement savings account already have a checking account. So the process of guiding your customers to a checking account means either moving their existing checking account to your bank or realizing that they already have a checking account. If the reason for their wanting the statement savings account is to create a forced savings vehicle, you will want to know where that money is coming from.

"Now is this monthly input coming from your checking account?"

"Yes it is."

"If that checking account is with us, we can handle the monthly input automatically. That might be easier for you."

"Yes. I never thought of that. We'll just take it out of my checking account."

Putting money in the savings account this way is similar to a direct deposit. And once you know where that checking account is, you can either build on it or transfer it to your bank, then build on it.

CD to Checking/Savings to ATM

CDs have become a wildly fluctuating financial service. If you remember, in 1983–84, CDs were an easy item to sell because the rates were so high. Many customers were coming into the bank and purchasing two-year CDs at 12 1/2 percent. By 1986, when many of those CDs reached maturity, those pleased customers returned to your bank and said, "I would like to roll over my $20,000 CD at the same rate as before."

"And what rate was that?" you kindly asked.

"12 1/2 percent."

You swallowed quickly. Your eyes might have bulged a bit. Then you ashamedly replied, "I'm sorry, Ma'am, but the best we can offer is 6 1/4 percent." Some bankers were able to convince their customers to roll their CDs over at 6 1/4 percent—back in 1986. Some rolled them over for two years. By 1988, CD rates were 5 percent. By 1990, they were 4 percent. And by 1992, rates had plummeted to 3 percent.

Remember?

That's a nice exaggeration. And I am sure it did happen to some of us. I ran into many situations where it started out that way, but because I anticipated the reaction, I was able to overcome the sales rejection. In general, and without respect to CD rates, the sales path of a CD would be determined by the customer's need to either live on the interest from the certificate or to use the interest to build on the equity.

In many instances, senior citizens are living on the interest from their investments. They will need a savings or checking account into which that monthly interest should be deposited. Many over 65 customers prefer a savings account while the under 65 might use a checking account. One should try to explain the benefits of an ATM card to those customers who elect to have a checking account. Sadly, most are afraid that they will get their fingers caught in the machine or refuse to listen to the benefits.

My mother is 80. We were talking about ATMs not too long ago. I asked her if she knew what an ATM was.

"Of course," she replied indignantly. "But they don't work."

"Don't work?" I asked puzzled.

"Absolutely. Your father and I were in Florida last spring and we decided we would use the darned thing to pay for our dinner. The restaurant refused it. We threw it away, after that."

Yes, there are still people who don't know what ATMs are.

IRA to Direct Deposit to Savings to ATM to Checking

Selling *off of* IRAs is a difficult thing to teach "on a universal level" since different financial institutions carry many different funding vehicles for an IRA. Some banks carry IRA CDs or IRA money funds. Some banks have IRA savings accounts where you can automatically have a certain amount of money taken from your pay check and deposited into your IRA. When it reaches the $2,000 figure, the account is "swept" and the contents used to open an IRA.

So, rather than discussing the various versions of the IRA product, let's focus on the concept of a tax-exempt retirement account that can be funded automatically. The restriction is that you can't take the money out of that account until you are fifty-nine-and-one-half without incurring tax penalties. So from that point of view we could refer to it as a retirement program.

Don't become confused over the word "retirement" because that word applies to the 40 and over market. What about the 29-year-old male wearing the gold necklace and driving a bright red Corvette? Is he interested in retirement? Of course not. According to him, he's gonna be dead by the time he's 40! He is interested in tax sheltering. That can still be done automatically through the bank accessing his checking account each month and building toward the maximum $2,000.

This sales path creates a forced mechanism to put aside money. A customer is looking for a way to put tax-free money aside. It can be done automatically, insuring that it will be done. An IRA can be created automatically from a special savings account which it will fund on a monthly basis from a checking account.

Money Market Account to ATM to Direct Deposit to CD to Savings

Either MMDA or MMA, they are still basically the same. Limited checking accounts returning higher interest than a NOW account. This is an upscale-customer account. The astute retail banker already knows that many customers have checking accounts and only write a few checks each month. They keep large balances (over $2,000) in those checking accounts.

A good retail bank salesperson will find his or her MMA customers in the disguise of checking (or current) account customers. Once the benefits of the MMA have been explained, the logical ATM card is introduced to allow access to cash without writing checks (since MMAs limit the customer to a low number of checks). Since many MMA customers are the Seniors Market, it is easy to understand how safely and quickly one's social security check can be automatically deposited via Direct Deposit. And once the customer is in that mind-set (of automatic deposits), other income (from annuities or investments) can be automatically deposited into a savings accounts or CDs.

Installment Loan to Auto Payment to Checking to ATM to Direct Deposit

Conceptually, the retail banker should understand how loans (asset-based products) create further needs for checking, savings, etc., (liability-based products). This is important to understand since the way retail banks make money is to balance their assets *and* liabilities and to grow the bank *evenly.*

For years, most community banks separated the lending and deposit-gathering functions to the point that the two were actually alienated in many banks—a condition that still prevalent today. More recently, bankers are beginning to realize that they must create a low-level lending authority for their sales staff, thus increasing the prospects for balanced growth. With technology advancements in the area of credit records, providing this limited lending authority is becoming increasingly more possible and more effective.

Let's create a realistic sales situation illustrating this balance: A customer approaches a salesperson who sells both deposits and loans. The customer explains that she wants to borrow $800 for a bedroom suite. That dollar figure is within the lending authority of the salesperson. Now, logically, anyone who loans money wants to make sure that they get the money back, so ability to re-pay is paramount. That concept will naturally guide the discussion with the customer. The salesperson finds out that the customer is a sales representative for a major "Fortune 500" firm and has just been transferred into the territory. She gives the banker her business card and together, the banker and the customer fill out the loan application. The bank salesperson has a "gut" feel is that she is legitimate.

So the process is fairly simple:

The banker knows that if he gets the customer's checking account he can have her monthly payment automatically deducted from her paycheck. According to the loan application she can certainly afford the monthly payments. So the banker will cross-sell an automatic payment *off of* the loan. The automatic payment will be made from the second cross-sold product: a checking account. When the customer signs for her checking account, she will sign for an ATM card which is "standard equipment on our checking account." The final cross-sold product of that sales situation should be a direct deposit relationship . . . so she doesn't have to stand in line to deposit her paycheck.

One first account and four second accounts!!

The success of this sale or any other will depend on your ability to "probe" properly and to build and maintain a level of trust with your customer.

Each of *your* lead products should be analyzed and a sales path developed. Use the Lead Product charts to identify your particular sales environment from a product and customer point of view.

The Sales Process

Selling in any retail establishment is extremely volatile. Banking is no different. Customers have established patterns and their banking habits are part of those patterns. Some days there are eight to ten customers waiting to see a banker and other days that bank salesperson can sit at his desk for three to four hours without one customer.

That volatility is called *Tuesday Selling versus Thursday Selling*. Tuesdays (generally) are very slow and Thursdays are hectic. Salespeople learn to sell differently depending on the amount of traffic. There are even times that are so busy that you don't have time to sell at all—just take orders.

On Thursdays you will need some "short cuts" to take in the selling process. On Tuesdays you should take your time and cultivate a relationship with your customers. Do some planning with them. Share ideas and make appointments. Also use Tuesdays for making telephone calls and follow-ups.

Some branches are busier than other branches and bank selling, in general, is feast or famine. With that in mind, let's take a look at a total sales process so that we can get an overview of the selling process and see where the sales paths we just discussed fit.

Let's choose a sales model patterned closely after our model in earlier chapters that would represent a functional process within a retail banking environment. It would consist of the following parts:

THE SALES MODEL

    I. PRE-SALES PLANNING

    II. INTRODUCTION

    III. NEEDS ANALYSIS

    IV. NEEDS FULFILLMENT

    V. CLOSE

    VI. FOLLOW-UP

In Figure 11.1 we presented The Sales Cycle.

This Sales Cycle is actually an exploded view of steps II to IV of the above mentioned Sales Model. We have isolated those parts of the sales model because research has shown us that in order to understand how to sell in a retail bank, one must learn *how to get started and what products to sell.* The Sales Cycle highlights the beginning process and incorporates the Sales Path (under "match related products to needs").

The Beginning of the Sale

The actual beginning of the sale occurs when the customer approaches the salesperson sitting at his desk and asks a question. That is where the action starts. And that is where most "order-takers" lose multiple product sales opportunities.

We have learned that for every 120 people who approach the desk of a salesperson, approximately 40 are interested in opening an account. Those forty are buyers.

They either want to open an account, or they have a question about an account, or they are having trouble with an existing account. They approach the salesperson and ask the first question.

Let's think about those questions. Let's think about exactly what their words are:

"Excuse me, I'd like some information on your checking accounts."

"I got a per-check charge on my last statement and I read that your checking accounts didn't charge for checks. Is that true?"

"Can you tell me your mortgage rates?"

"I need some information on your college loans."

"How much money do I have to put into one of those IRA's?"

"Why do you people constantly keep charging me for over-drawing my account when I am not over-drawn?"

"Yeah. I need to buy a car. Can you give me some information on financing?"

"I've lost my social security check. What do I do?"

"What are your hours, anyway? Everytime I need cash you guys are closed."

"Who do I talk to about mutual funds?"

"Can I pay for my electricity here?"

"Can you help me change the names on my savings accounts?"

In any sales situation it is important that the sales person be in control of the sales communication. This is done by the salesperson asking the questions. That poses a problem for the retail banker whose customer (in almost every case) asks the first question.

That problem is solved when the salesperson learns to answer questions with a question. It is called *the question/question technique*. This is not an evasive thing to do. If it sounds evasive, then you are doing it wrong. When you do it right, it changes the momentum of the sales encounter.

When a customer asks you a question the momentum is going from the customer to the salesperson. If you start by answering that question, all you are doing is adding to the current momentum of the encounter.

A sales encounter has the momentum going from the sales person to the customer, not from the customer to the sales person. That point is extremely important.

The person asking the questions is the person in charge of the encounter.

Without that knowledge, here is how it might work:

Situation A

Customer:	"I'd like some information on your checking accounts."
Banker:	"I'd be happy to tell you about them. We have a Minimum Balance Checking and a Flat-Fee Checking. The Minimum Balance Checking account is called our Super Standard. It requires that you keep a $1,000 minimum balance in your account. If you do, there is no monthly service charge. Our Flat-Fee Checking Account requires no minimum balance, but you will pay a monthly charge of $6.00. Which one would you like?"

That is called *Tell Selling*. The banker simply reacted to the momentum of the customer. Tell Selling is when the sales person does the talking.

Situation B is called *Ask Selling*. It utilizes the concept of the question/question to reverse the momentum.

Situation B

Customer:	"I'd like some information on your checking account."
Banker:	"Are you familiar with our checking accounts?"
Customer:	"No. Not really."

Banker:	"Are you used to keeping a minimum balance in your checking account?"
Customer:	"Yeah. My old bank made me keep $1,000 in there."
Banker:	"Did they pay you interest on that money?"
Customer:	"Not that I know of. Should they?"
Banker:	"If you keep $1,000 in a checking account with us, we will pay you 3 1/2 percent. "

Ask Selling is when the customer does the talking.

In Situation A, the banker responded to the customer—answered his/her question. In Situation B, the customer responded to the banker who probed in a non-offensive way by answering a question with a question.

The instant that the customer said "Checking Account," the astute banker should have visualized the lead product sales path. Then the banker would have known how to progress with the multiple product sale. You can go through this visualization process regardless of whether it is Tuesday or Thursday.

The important part of this lead product concept is knowing exactly what words you will use. You should define those words for the lead product and each of the cross-sales. The first words come from the customer. They are the question. The next words come from the bank salesperson. They are the *question/question*. Then a series of predictable questions take place.

Let's take a closer look at Situation B, constructing a parallel analysis and illustrating the sales path as well as the question/question and the following sales probes:

CHECKING

The Question

Customer: I'd like some information on your checking account.

The Question/Question

Banker: Are you familiar with our checking accounts?

Customer: No. Not really.

Probe for existing account info

Banker: Are you used to keeping a minimum balance in your checking account?

Customer: Yeah. My old bank made me keep $1,000 in there.

Banker: Did they pay you interest on that money?

Customer: Not that I know of. Should they?

The Value of the Product

Banker: If you keep $1,000 in a checking account with us, we will pay you 3 1/2 percent.

Trial Closing

Banker: Does that sound like it would be of interest to you?

Customer:	Well, yeah. Better than my present checking account

Confirming the benefits

Banker:	Tell me, Mr. Gabriel, how many checks do you write each month? A lot?
Customer:	No. Actually very few. . . maybe four or five.

Closing the Sale

Banker:	Well, it sounds to me like our Super Standard Checking Account will be a big improvement over your other one. Was that account local?
Customer:	No. I'm just moving here from Durango, Colorado.
	The Banker assists the customer in filling out the new account registration.
Banker:	Well, Mr. Gabriel, you're all taken care of. If you just sign here and here. . . Then sign here.

Implied Sale

Customer:	What is this third signature for?

ATM

Banker:	That's for your ATM card. It's standard equipment on our Super Standard Checking Account. And it's free.
Customer:	Well, that's good. There's hardly anything free these days.

Probe for Direct Deposit

Banker:	Are you working locally, Mr. Gabriel?
Customer:	Sort of. I'm selling for Procter & Gamble and this is my territory.

DIRECT DEPOSIT

Banker:	That is a very fine company and you'll love this territory. The reason I asked is that your paycheck can be automatically transferred into the bank if you want. That way you don't have to stand in the kind of line you see over there.
Customer:	That's a good idea. I didn't even think of that. How do I go about doing that?
Banker:	It's very easy. I'll take care of it for you. All you have to do is sign this card.
Customer:	That's very convenient. I appreciate that.

Probe for Savings Account

SAVINGS ACCOUNT

Banker: I'm happy to be able to help out. You
know, Mr. Gabriel, since you are moving
out here and you have our checking account and ATM card, you might be interested in the fact that our ATM card can
link your checking account to your savings
account. That means you can take money
out of one account and put it in another by
using just your card. Do you presently
have a savings account in Durango?

Customer: As a matter of fact I do. I guess it's not
going to be very accessible out there, uh?

Banker: Not really. If you sign here I can make arrangements to have your savings funds
transferred to a statement savings account
with us.

Learning to sell "off of" other products is a key concept in
financial products selling. This concept is helpful on busy
Thursdays and Fridays because it allows the salesperson to interact quickly and efficiently with the customer. On Mondays
and Tuesdays the salesperson can spend more time learning the
customer's real financial needs, still using the sales path as a
guide.

The sales encounter described previously resulted in one first account and three second accounts. It was done through questioning and relating products. Figure 11.4 tracks that encounter for you.

The following activities have been developed to allow you to create your own sales path and to construct beginning sales encounter dialogue.

Figure 11.4

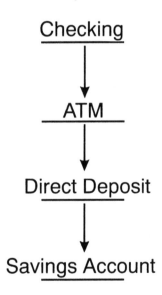

Checking

ATM

Direct Deposit

Savings Account

Figure 11.5

Below are listed some questions that an average customer might ask. Write the question/question that you would ask plus the Lead Product Sales Path.

1.

Question   Customer: Can you tell me your
                              mortgage rates?

Question/   Banker: Are you interested in a fixed-rate
Question   or adjustable-rate mortgage?

Sales Path

Figure 11.6

2.

Question   Customer: I'd like some information on
your Certificates.

Question/   _____
Question   _____
_____

Sales Path

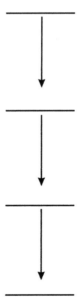

Figure 11.7

3.

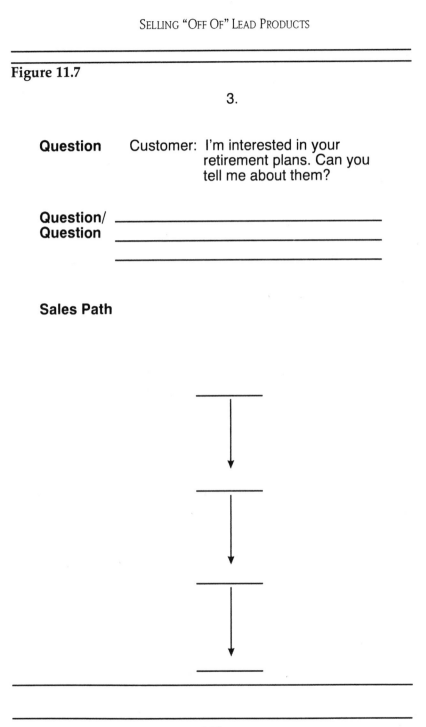

Question   Customer: I'm interested in your
retirement plans. Can you
tell me about them?

Question/
Question

Sales Path

Figure 11.8

4.

Question   Customer: I'm looking for different
alternatives in terms of
funding my daughter's
education.

Question/   _____
Question   _____

_____

Sales Path

Personal Needs, Financial Needs and Related Products

Actually, Lead Product Selling does not take into consideration the true needs of the customer. Salespeople use it when they are busy, or as a guide line . . . a direction to go with a customer.

Real selling involves a sensitivity to the customer's needs; his or her personal needs, and financial needs. To identify these determinations, we must be able to listen carefully to what our customers are telling us. Usually what they are saying is one thing while their needs are another.

Customers with a strong parental obligation will spend an inordinant amount of time talking about their children. As their children reach their teens, those strongly parent-oriented customers think in terms of services whose benefits satisfy their need for parental obligation.

Translated into financial needs, many families are talking extended credit, or forced savings.

Unlike Maslow's Theory of Hierarchy, the following approach to needs involves seven basic humanistic needs that relate smoothly to the banking industry; and one does not need to satisfy one need to move on to the next. But, like Maslow's, these needs are prioritized from the most basic to the most complex.

The chart on the next page illustrates the personal, and financial needs and the products that tie into them.

Determining the financial products and services that customers need requires that the salesperson knows the customers and makes them feel comfortable so the salesperson can correctly choose the products that will fulfill the customers' personal and financial needs.

An elderly customer deeply concerned about making ends meet on a fixed income is looking for retirement money. But, more important, that person wants to live with dignity and it is

Sales Needs Grid		
PERSONAL NEEDS	**FINANCIAL NEEDS**	**PRODUCTS**
1. Basic utility	Ease of handling/ convenience	Checking, ATM, convenience banking products
2. Personal goods and services	High interest checking	Money market account
3. Parental obligation	Extended credit	GSL, Plus, equity credit
4. Astuteness	Tax avoidance	Retirement Accounts
5. Security	Financial advice	CDs, discount brokerage, etc.
6. Status	Credit	Mortgage, loans

the desire for dignity that dictates how we, as salespersons, must interact with that customer.

Customers who come in because they don't know whether to roll over a CD or get out of certificates and get into a mutual fund—or whatever—are looking for some financial advice because they are concerned about the security of their investment.

Most car loans are status loans, unless the customer is buying the cheapest car available. Even though many customers appear unencumbered by the personal needs listed in the chart, it is the intuitive salesperson who understands what makes his customers buy.

SUMMARY

1. Lead Product Selling is learning to sell "off of" certain lead products.

2. For the average retail bank salesperson, 50 percent of their first accounts will be checking, 15 percent savings, 15 percent CDs and 20 percent miscellaneous.

3. Sometimes retail bank salespeople are so busy on Thursdays and Fridays that selling is almost impossible. That's why visualizing lead products is helpful.

4. On Mondays and Tuesdays the salesperson can spend a lot of time with his customers. He can find out, in an in-depth way, many of their financial needs. The lead product sales path is then a helpful guide.

5. A sales encounter should have the customer answering questions and the salesperson asking questions.

6. The right product for the right customer involves separating Personal Needs from Financial Needs. The style or mood of the communication would be dictated by the personal needs of the customer. The practical part of the communication would involve the financial needs.

Chapter TWELVE

LEAD PRODUCT SELLING IN NON-RETAIL BANKING SITUATIONS

The concept of cross-selling works in all of the financial and fiduciary services. It also links financial services to fiduciary services. That linking process is what has brought legal and accounting services into the overall financial services market—from a marketing and sales point of view.

Because the world of investment services has become so broad, retail bankers must understand what their competition is like, from a sales point of view. Elsewhere in this book we discussed the birth and growth of the mutual funds industry. Because they are classified as investment services, they are sold in a manner which is familiar to the retail banker.

The environment and the salespeople are different than the environment and sales personnel of a retail bank. The biggest difference is in the amount of information the salespeople are expected to know in the mutual funds business. Secondly, most selling of mutual funds is done over the telephone.

Training for Mutual Funds Selling

Mutual funds sales personnel have been trained in the concept of investments—trained in the theories of how to invest. Retail bank salespeople are trained to learn products—percentage return on CDs. Mutual funds salespeople, for the most part, understand the stock market; they can discuss total return in a variety of investment products and services; they have access, through their own computers, to stock information and competitive mutual funds. The mutual funds salesperson has been trained in the total delivery process much better than the retail bank salesperson.

Many small community banks create an alliance with an investment company to provide an investment specialist who resides at the bank. The retail salespeople refer investment clients to the specialists. In some cases this works well. In most cases, however, the retail bank fails to train their personnel in how to make investment referrals, so the investment specialist must create his or her own market. Many retail bank salespeople see the investment specialist as competition to their own investment products: certificates of deposit and savings accounts . . . even savings bank life insurance.

The larger banks have developed their own mutual funds and in many cases have re-trained their retail staff to be able to sell the new product. Earlier chapters were designed to give the average retail salesperson enough information to understand the retail investment market enough to be curious. There are many books and videos available today which can provide a more in-depth look at this market. One of the most user-friendly books I have read is *The Wall Street Journal Guide to Understanding Money Markets*. This booklet clearly and graphically explains the various investment vehicles.

Interestingly enough, selling mutual funds and selling CDs are very similar:

1. A customer asks a question.
2. The salesperson asks a question/question.
3. The salesperson confirms the financial needs of the customer.

Where the mutual funds salesperson excels is step 3. Here the mutual funds salesperson needs to find out the objectives of the customer, why the customer wants a particular fund.

The following mutual fund sales dialogue will illustrate this:

The phone rings at the desk of Kate Hollister, a sales representative for a major mutual fund:

"Good afternoon, Kate Hollister. May I help you?"

"Yes. I want to buy your Byzantine Fund. How do I go about doing this?"

"It's very simple. May I have your name?"

"Yes. Arnold Kruzinger."

"Mr. Kruzinger, are you aware of the fund's performance?"

Kate Hollister can now refer to the customer by name and she has turned the momentum of the conversation around by asking a question/question.

"Absolutely. I've watched it for the past six months and read a recent article on it in *Money* magazine. I think its total return was around 11 percent last year."

"I'll tell you exactly what it was."

We hear her bringing it up on her computer. "Eleven point eight-seven."

"Yeah. It sounds like what I'm looking for."

"So high return is what you are looking for?" She is obviously confirming his financial needs.

"You bet. I'm interested in making money."

"Is this going to be a long-term investment, Mr. Kruzinger?"

She is now making the customer clarify his objectives.

"Well . . . until I'm fifty-nine and a half."

"So it's a retirement program?"

"Sort of. I'm just putting money away until then."

"Do you have a retirement program where you work?"

She now realizes the customer might not know enough about retirement programs to make a totally competent decision.

"No. That's why I need to put money away."

"So you are familiar with IRAs?"

"Oh, yeah. I've been funding those through my bank for the past five years."

"That sounds like you're well on your way to retirement planning, Mr. Kruzinger."

"Is this Byzantine Fund a retirement fund?"

"Not really. Tell me, have you funded your IRA for this year?"

"Two thousand for me and two thousand for Mary."

"Mary's your wife?"

"Yeah. We both put our maximum contribution away."

"The reason I asked about whether you and your wife have funded your IRA this year is because the Byzantine Fund might not be what you're looking for."

"You mean you think you can do better than 11 percent?"

The previous sales dialogue is interesting for a retail sales-person to read. It makes the retail banker realize the importance of product knowledge—not only knowledge of the products that retail banks offer, but knowledge of products that are offered by mutual funds and brokerages. As the banking industry becomes more efficient with a broader range of investment products, they will begin to make larger in-roads into the over-all financial services market.

To further illustrate the relationship sales techniques in this broad industry which includes trust companies, law firms, and international financial services, the following sales dialogue will once again show the importance of product knowledge, and the importance of understanding the financial needs of the customer.

First some background: In many of the large harbors tucked into the lush islands of the tropical Caribbean, one sees an endless number of yachts. Some of these yachts cost just under $100,000 while some can cost $10 million. The curious financial/fiduciary salesperson might wonder about these owners. What are they like? What businesses are they in?

There is a lot of inherited wealth floating around the Caribbean. But in larger numbers are very successful entrepreneurs who have learned the legal ins-and-outs of converting business money into personal comfort—doing this in an absolutely legal manner. It is done through the varied tax laws of the countries who govern the islands and countries in the Caribbean, Central and South America. Many of these countries allow their citizens to establish businesses and/or residences in tax-friendly neighboring countries. These citizens, through the use of very bright attorneys' can minimize their tax liabilities thus enabling them to have more money to spend on luxuries: yachts, villas, etc.

Even though the U.S. is one of the most strict, inflexible governments in terms of allowing excessive tax advantages, the U.S. government did establish the U.S. Virgin Islands as a tax-friendly possession where savvy exporters can minimize taxes in their business.

We now meet Mr. Roberto Salvat, a wealthy entrepreneur, living in South America. He has just closed on the purchase of a $5 million yacht. One of the draw-backs to this purchase is that his government will not allow him enough tax advantages to support the maintenance of the craft. Since an expensive yacht would require sizable maintenance expenses such as salaries for the skipper, chef and full crew plus fuel, dockage fees, etc.; the owner can treat his yacht like a corporation with legitimate expenses and taxes. Mr. Salvat's lawyer has recommended that he create an International Business Company (IBC) in a tax friendly jurisdiction. Mr. Salvat is familiar with the development of off-shore companies and contacts a well-known trust company in the British Virgin Islands. His call is referred to Maurice Werner, one of the managing directors.

"I need to speak with someone about forming a corporation for a yacht."

"I will let you speak with Mr. Maurice Werner, our managing director."

"This is Maurice Werner."

"Yes, Mr. Werner. My name is Robert Salvat. I am enquiring about setting up a company that would own a luxury ship I have just agreed to purchase."

"I'm sure we can handle that for you, Mr. Salvat. Tell me a little about your yacht."

Just like in retail bank selling, the fiduciary salesperson begins the sales conversation with a question/question. That turns the control of the sales encounter over to the salesperson.

The next questions he asks will qualify Mr. Salvat in a variety of categories: the kind of yacht, estimated maintenance costs, the owner's citizenship.

And just like retail banking services, we can review the sales path. The lead product was the International Business Company. The related services (the sales path) were:

1. ship registration

2. checking account

3. credit card.

In the future, Mr. Werner will contact Mr. Salvat to make sure everything is running smoothly because Mr. Salvat will need more trust and investment advice. Many non-banking services—yet still financially related services—are becoming part of an overall service. It is no longer a series of separate businesses: banking, trust companies, law firms, accountants.

Today—and the trend for the future—is making the concept of related products become one package.

SUMMARY

1. The concept of cross-selling links financial services to fiduciary services.

2. Mutual funds sales personnel have been trained in the concept of investments; trained in the theories of how to invest. Retail bank salespeople are trained to memorize products.

3. Many community banks create an alliance with an investment company to provide an investment specialist who resides at the bank.

4. The larger banks have developed their own mutual funds and in many cases have re-trained their retail staff to be able to sell the new product.

5. Selling mutual funds, fiduciary services and CDs are very similar:

   a. A customer asks a question.

   b. The salesperson asks a question/question.

   c. The salesperson confirms the financial needs of the customer.

Section FOUR

Case Studies

Chapter THIRTEEN

CONTINUUM: ACTIVITY AND CASE STUDY

It's now time to put some of the material we covered in earlier sections of this book into action, so that you can see how much of what we've covered you have absorbed. We'll start by returning to our Formal/Informal Continuum

Let's assume you are a banker sitting at your desk. You see a customer coming across the lobby. It is a woman in a striking grey business suit. She is carrying a small cordovan attaché case in one hand and has *The Wall Street Journal* tucked under her other arm. She appears to be in her late thirties—maybe early forties. Her hair is carefully styled and streaked with grey. Something about her tells you she is in a rush.

Where does she belong on the continuum? Is your first impression of her one of formality or informality? Obviously this customer is formal. How formal? Is she the most formal person you have ever seen? Probably not. She might be, say, a 3.

Now where is your 5? If you have analyzed your behavior and the characteristics that make up your behavior, you will present yourself just a little bit to the left of 5—a little more formal. If you have not learned the concept of finding your 5, you will be at the mercy of your customer—constantly defending your behavior. The following example should illustrate this dilemma. On the continuum in phase one of this exercise we might want to place the customer as follows:

Formal   Informal

1   3   5   7   10

Now let's use, as the bank employee, a male in his late 40s whose top button under his tie is never buttoned; who looks for the opportunity to take off his suit coat; whose shoes continually reflect his rural interests; whose hair is short but not styled; who loves to joke around with his customers. Let's put that salesperson on the continuum with our woman in the grey suit. As you can see there is a significant distance between their two personalities; the customer is a 3 and the banker is a 7. The

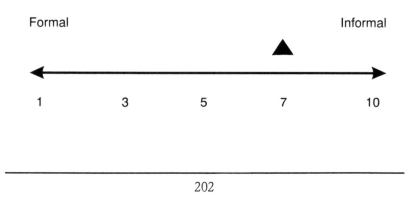

Formal   Informal

1   3   5   7   10

distance between those two behaviors we will call The Degree of Discomfort. And we can determine numerically that the degree is actually four (7 minus 3). As long as the salesman maintains his behavior and the customer maintains hers, neither will reach a level of comfort conducive to relationship selling.

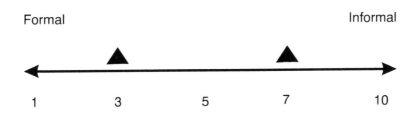

Formal   Informal

1   3   5   7   10

To create a sales environment the salesman will have to make some changes which will put the customer at ease; i.e., to narrow the degree of discomfort. It isn't the customer's job to be more receptive to improved communications. It is the bank employee's.

This situation could have been avoided in the first place if the salesman would have analyzed his own behavior and made the kind of adjustment necessary for him to present himself as a 5—reducing the degree of discomfort to a more tolerable 2.

A Group Activity for the Continuum Numbering System

To determine what number you actually are (within the eyes of other people) create a group activity as follows:

Pick ten people who work with you. Explain the Formal/Informal Continuum to them using the material presented earlier in this book.

Ask them who they think is the most formal and the most informal. Give them some suggestions: Queen Elizabeth, Richard

Pryor, etc. Explain the numbering system carefully. Verify your explanation by asking everyone to write down a number which best describes Richard Nixon. Have them pass all of the numbers to you. Write the numbers on a flip chart. It will look like this:

3

2

4

1

3

2

8

2

2

1

Now you can see that one person in your group (the person who gave Nixon an "8") either wasn't listening or has some very strange ideas about formal behavior.

He or she will probably say they got confused and meant "2." Make the change, total all the numbers and divide by 10. Richard Nixon is a "2.2." Some perceive that level of formality as "1" and some as "4." Each person would adjust their own behavior accordingly if they were to sell financial or fiduciary services to Mr. Nixon!

Now that your group understands the concept, tell them you would like to have them rate a few more personalities. You are going to have them rate each other, but don't tell them that or they will start thinking about the numbers in advance. You want spontaneous decisions—their first impressions.

Pass out a piece of paper that looks like Figure 13.1.

Figure 13.1

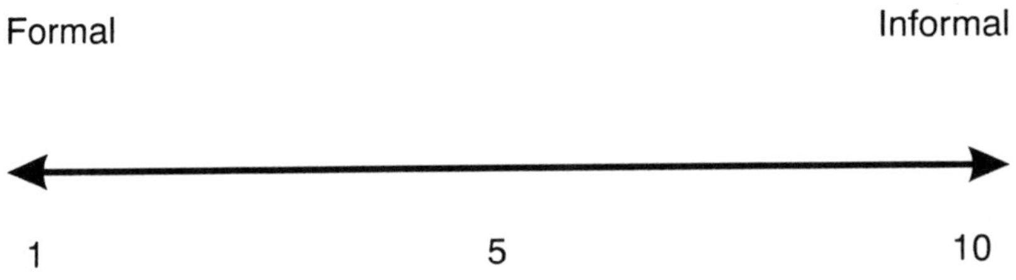

Formal   Informal

1   5   10

                    1.
                    2.
                    3.
                    4.
                    5.
                    6.
                    7.
                    8.
                    9.
                 10.

With this piece of paper in front of them ask them one more time if they understand the rules. Then from a prepared list read off the name of each person in your group.

After you read the name of the first person, stop and explain to everyone that they should also rate themselves. Then continue, allowing about two seconds between each name.

The rest of this exercise should take about ten minutes.

Figure 13.2 is very helpful for the analysis stage of this activity.

You had previously made a list of the ten members of your group. You read the names in the order on that list. That order should be put on the above work sheet. It should be listed vertically and horizontally.

Now you should copy the numbers from the ten pieces of paper that each member of your group filled out. *Always copy the numbers onto this grid horizontally so you can total them vertically.*

You will end up with a matrix that has everyone's name in the far left-hand column and across the top (in the same order). You will also have the numbers that correspond to each person that you have recorded, horizontally.

Now just total the columns vertically and divide by ten.

Figure 13.3 is a matrix from one of my seminars. I have changed the names. Let's look at it together. The circled numbers are the ones indicating how each person rated themselves. The squares along the bottom of the grid are the averages of the numbers that each person gave to each individual.

Some of us see ourselves accurately. Others do not. My experience shows that the more extreme one's behavior, the further apart the average is from that individual's personal assessment. Most people who think they are "9s" come out as "7s." But those people who think they are "5s" generally average out as "5s" . . . or very close to it.

Good sales people are honest with themselves. They know how they appear in the eyes of other people. So an important step in developing a sales personality is to analyze yourself and your impact on and relation to other people. How good a first impression do you make? Is it the same impression after several visits?

Figure 13.2

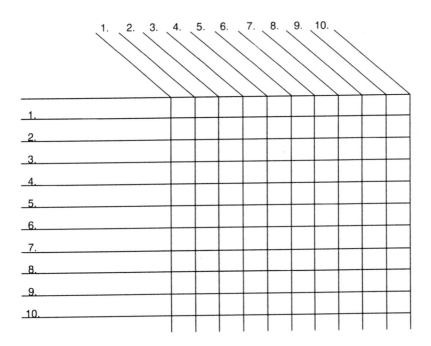

Figure 13.3

	1. Johnson	2. Cargas	3. Haas	4. Foreman	5. Garfield	6. Morton	7. Tilden	8. Weber	9. Hutton	10. Ferris
1. Johnson	(7)	5	6	4	3	4	8	2	7	5
2. Cargas	4	(6)	6	5	4	5	8	3	7	4
3. Haas	4	5	(5)	5	4	4	7	3	6	4
4. Foreman	6	6	5	(4)	3	5	7	4	6	5
5. Garfield	4	5	6	7	(2)	5	9	6	7	2
6. Morton	5	5	5	5	4	(4)	6	5	6	5
7. Tilden	4	5	5	6	4	5	(7)	6	7	5
8. Weber	3	6	6	6	5	5	7	(5)	6	5
9. Hutton	5	6	6	5	4	5	6	5	(6)	4
10. Ferris	4	5	5	6	5	5	7	4	5	(3)
	4.6	5.4	5.5	5.3	3.8	4.9	7.2	4.3	6.3	4.2

Selling is not just telling people what the products are and asking if they want it. That is a very naive view of selling. Your ability to understand human behavior is of primary importance. More important than product knowledge. More important than some sales model.

People buy from people with whom they feel comfortable.

A Sales Communications Case Study

The following case study was developed in a retail banking sales format. As we move through this study, I will make judgements and comments relating it back to what we have just learned.

The bank sales person is named Fran Willis. She is in her late thirties and has been with the bank for ten years. She came up "through the ranks" . . . teller, head teller, Customer Service Representative and now she is Customer Service Supervisor. She works in a busy branch. There are two full-time Customer Service Representatives, plus herself. Fran is averaging 65 first accounts per month.

It is a normal Wednesday afternoon. The branch is moderately busy. As Fran looks around she shows the strain of last night's intense argument with her husband, Ben. Both Nancy and Ed, her two Customer Service Representatives, are busy with what appear to be routine customers.

Fran feels good about her early morning meeting with her branch manager. They discussed the sales ratios in the branch. Her manager apologized that they had to meet on a Wednesday morning before the branch opened but she would be out on Saturday and unable to conduct the weekly branch sales meeting. Fran had to do it. She looks forward to these meetings and feels like the sales manager of the branch, anyway. Her ratio is consistently over 1.90. The fact that Nancy's ratio has been as high as 2.61 speaks well for Fran's ability to manage her CSRs. In the beginning, Fran was disturbed that Nancy's ratio was higher than hers, but as she got into the new sales culture, she learned that the best sales person is not always the sales manager. She remembered the meeting she had with Todd Ellison, the VP in charge of retail banking. He told her that having the highest ratio could be equated to being the "fastest gun in the west"—someday someone was going to come along and beat you. But the longer that "fast gun" lived, it meant that someone was organizing and protecting him. Otherwise, he'd be dead. Fran learned she was the organizer and protector. Yet she knew she also had to be above average with her ratio and it should be consistent.

Her thoughts were suddenly halted as she focused in on a new customer approaching her desk. At the same time, she saw Mrs. Berman (a long time customer of the bank) enter the lobby holding some papers in her hands; and she noticed one of the tellers directing a customer to her.

"Uh oh," she thought. "It seems that everything happens in spurts."

The customer approaching her was in his mid to late thirties (she guessed). He was wearing a "well done" gray business suit and carrying an attaché case.

"Looks like a perfect '3'," she thought as she stood up to greet him.

"Good morning, I'm Fran Willis. May I help you?" she said, realizing the importance of starting the communication.

"Yeah. I'm Mike Whish. I'm concerned about all these different kinds of checking accounts and whether I have the right one . . . "Sit down, Mr. Whish. Let me see if I can help you." Fran said, motioning to the chair.

In Fran's mind, she is now trying to figure out whether he is a customer of her bank with a problem or a customer of another bank and is beginning to realize he has the wrong account. She did notice that he gave her a firm handshake which could indicate he is perceiving her as an equal. Many men shake women's hands very loosely which indicates (psychologically) that they don't want to harm the female. And that translates into the male perceiving the female in a non-important, submissive role.

"Tell me, Mr. Whish," Fran continues. "Are you a customer of our bank?"

"No. I could be, though. I was talking with a friend of mine who is earning interest on his checking account. In my last statement I discovered I was earning none."

"Do you know what kind of checking account you have?"

"I dunno," he shrugged. "A checking account checking account." He smiled a bit apologetically. "I know that sounds stupid."

"Not at all, Mr. Whish. You are going through what a lot of people are, in regards to financial services. There are new products daily, and, quite often, the customer is the last to know."

He leaned back in the chair and crossed his legs. Fran noticed, for the first time that she was beginning to define his comfort level. He wasn't really a "3"; more like a "5" or "6." She knew that he was looking to her for information. At this point, she wanted to make sure that she didn't take on an advisory role until he gave her further signs of trust.

"Tell me. Do you usually keep at least $700 in your account?"

"You mean after I write my rent check?"

"Yes."

Fran was beginning to feel more confident with this transaction. When Mr. Whish said "rent," that told Fran that he was
not a homeowner. Also it might indicate that his rent would
cover all utilities. "A strong possibility that he doesn't write a
lot of checks," she thought.

"Well, let me see," he pondered briefly. "I've never over-
drawn my account. Yes. I'd say I've always got at least $700 in
there. Why? Does it make a difference?"

"Oh, yes. Generally speaking, if you "zero out" at the end
of each month and you write a lot of checks, you probably won't
get any interest on your checking account. But if, as you seem to
indicate, you keep a reasonable minimum balance in your
checking account, you should be earning some interest."

"O.K.," Mr. Whish said. "Let me get this straight. Rule one
says that if I keep around $700 in my account . . ."

" . . . or something like that," Fran interrupted.

"Yeah," he shrugged, indicating the exact dollar amount
was not important. "Around $700. If I keep a high balance, I
should be earning something."

"That's right. Also, Mr. Whish . . ."

"Call me Mike," he interrupted, leaning forward and putting his elbow on Fran's desk.

A good sign for Fran. She consciously realized that she
made a significant step in closing a comfort level with Mike
Whish. The body language, the tone of his voice, and the suggestion to call him by his first name told Fran she was narrowing the Degree of Discomfort in the relationship.

Out of instinct, Fran noticed that Ed was not waiting on
anyone, and Mrs. Berman was sitting in the customer waiting
area appearing fidgety. This was the part of her job that she did
not like. It isn't just a matter of working with customers, one at
a time. Her sub-conscious mind was now dealing with Mike
Whish while her conscious mind was trying to figure out what

to do with Ed. Then her phone rang. She let it ring twice and looked around. "What in the world is wrong with Ed?" she thought, "Why doesn't he pick up the phone?"

"I'm sorry, Mike. Let me answer this. It will just take a second."

"Sure. Sounds like my office." He smiled. That made her feel better about the comfort level; he was identifying with her. "Good morning, Fran Willis."

"Hi Fran. Todd Ellison. Ya got a few minutes?"

That just about sent Fran through the ceiling. Remember Todd Ellison is the VP in charge of retail banking? "Have I got a couple of minutes?" she scoffed under her breath.

"Gee, Todd, I'm sorry. I'm with a customer right now. Can I call you back?" At that instant she saw Mrs. Berman stand up and put her hands on her hips, looking around for someone to help her. "Sure, Fran. I'll be here all morning," Todd said.

Fran hung up, keeping her eye on Mrs. Berman. "'Scuse me one second," she said as she got up, waving to Mrs. Berman. She stopped by Ed's desk and leaned close to his ear. "I can't believe you haven't seen Mrs. Berman sitting there or heard the telephone ringing! Either work here or don't!" she snapped. Then she motioned to Mrs. Berman.

"Mrs. Berman, I'm sorry you had to wait. Mr. Challis here is free now. Ed?" Then she walked off.

"I'm sorry, Mike. Mornings like this make me wish I was on the slow shift at the fire department."

"Don't worry about it."

Fran glanced down at the notes she had taken and was glad she had developed that discipline. "We were talking about the fact that if you keep $700 in your checking account you should be earning interest. And I agree. One other factor is the number of checks you write each month. If we had an idea of your minimum balance and the number of checks you write, we could talk about a variety of checking accounts that pay you interest."

"Number of checks? I dunno. Not very many."

"Does your rent include utilities?" she probed.

"Yeah. Just one check, there. And I get monthly expense checks from my business which covers food and so forth."

"What about meals and clothes?"

"Oh, I always use my VISA card."

"Insurance? Car payments? Any of those kinds of monthly checks?" she continued, feeling that he was working with her trying to solve his dilemma.

"My insurance is quarterly. I drive a company car. No alimony payments. Not married. Thank God!" he chuckled.

"It sounds like you're not writing more than three checks a month. You know, Mike, if you could discipline yourself to keep a couple of thousand in your checking account and write just three or less checks each month, you would qualify for our Preferred Money Market Account which gives you a higher return than a savings account, lets you write checks and charges you absolutely nothing in terms of fees.

Let's stop here and see how much attention you've been paying—and how good you are at addressing the needs of your customer. Try to answer these questions without going back and reading the case study. After you have answered them to the best of your ability, go back and read the case study.

1. What is the customer's name? _____

2. Is he married? _____

3. Who are the people who work for Fran Willis (first and last names, if available)? _____

   —_____

   _____

4. Does the customer have a checking account?

   _____

5. Do you think the customer has a savings account?
   Why? _____

   _____

   _____

6. What do you think the customer's personal needs are?

   _____

7. What are his financial needs? _____

   _____

8. Strictly as a personal "hunch" at this point in the sales
   encounter, what products should the customer have?

   _____

   _____

9. If Fran is successful in opening a Super NOW account,
   what are the related products in the Lead Product
   Sales Path? _____

   _____

10. If Fran is successful in opening a Super NOW account
    and three other accounts, what would be her ratio
    (just for that one customer)?_____

    _____

    _____

You'll really know if you've passed this "test" when you
deal with your next customer.

Chapter FOURTEEN

ANALYZING CASE STUDIES

In order to put a lot of what we have developed into practice, I have structured three case studies which illustrate sales communications between a banking customer and a platform person.

I've attempted to make the situations materially different and to make the personality of the sales person "show through" the case study. This was done by asking friends of ours who work in banks to write up situations they have encountered while selling in banks.

With headings and parenthetical comments, I have attempted to analyze the sale and relate it to the model as well as to specific parts of the book.

As you will notice, selling doesn't always happen in the proper order. Unfortunately our customers haven't been trained to be perfect customers. What we see is the "workable" model, one that is flexible and illustrates the problem solving ability of the sales person.

At times the salesperson will be probing for verification before he or she does any internalizing of a sales path. It might appear that the salesperson is "out of sync" with the model. In fact, what is happening is that the salesperson is being flexible and "bending" with the particular situation. The overall model is still intact. The broadest elements of the outline are in order. What you should learn is that a good salesperson treats each sale individually and gears his or her approach to the customer and to the situation. There is no set method that works all the time with everyone when it comes to behavioral situations.

Case Study #1

Background During June our bank had a certificate promotion. We offered a higher rate on short-term certificates than all other banks in our market. The bank imposed several rules on the customer. The minimum deposit would be $5,000.00; the maximum $100,000.00, and only open to residents or existing out-of-state customers. Our mission was to cross-sell everyone who came through the door. We were much busier than we anticipated and found it very hard to take the time to cross-sell with a lobby full of people waiting and wondering when it would be their turn.

Pre-Sales Planning An older couple came in and sat down. One of my tellers was instructed to greet the customers, offer them a cup of coffee and let them know there would be a short wait. They told her they were retired and didn't mind waiting.

Introduction   After they waited for 30 minutes, I was ready to help them. I went out to the lobby, introduced myself, learned their name was Smith, apologized for the wait and brought them over to my desk.

Product Inquiry   Their first words (and almost everyone else's during this promotion) were, "We're interested in a 6-month CD—is this really the rate?"

Pre-Sales Planning   I had decided prior to waiting on any customers that I would immediately get into the product, from a sales point of view, since the rate would create controversy and any "beating around the bush" would only create skepticism. After I assured them that the rate was real, they decided to purchase a 6-month CD.

Needs Analysis   I asked them if the proceeds from the CD were going to be part of their monthly living allowance. *(Financial Questioning)* They indicated, "Not necessarily." I took that to mean that they could live on their fixed income but if they needed some money it would be nice to know where it was. *(Internalizing Needs)* I suggested that compounding their interest would give them an even higher rate. They had no idea what that meant and frowned seriously at each other. I thought I was going to lose them. As briefly as possible, I explained with pencil and paper what compounding their interest would mean to them; exactly how much more money they would earn in six months. They liked that.

Needs Fulfillment   We pay simple interest on all of our certificates so I suggested to my customers that it would be beneficial to them to open a Money Market account or a savings account so that the interest earned on a CD would compound to give them a greater return on their money. They could have an interest check sent out monthly, but I have found the security and peace of mind derived from an actual account makes customers feel more at ease . . . not to mention the fact that statistics show that the more accounts a customer has with you, the lower the probability that they will change banks.

Needs Analysis   It turned out that the couple had just moved into the area from Connecticut and saw our certificates ad in the paper. After probing briefly to determine exactly where they lived I found out we were the closest bank to their new condominium. As I asked questions in order to open the CD, they told me all about their daughter and grandchildren who live in the area.

Needs Fulfillment   I was at the portion of the new account opening process that asks how the interest will be paid out. I went into the normal discussion about putting the interest into an interest bearing account; either a savings account or MMDA. The Smiths decided an MMDA would be appropriate for their needs—which I had previously probed for. (Verification) I made sure that they understood the limitations on an MMDA: that is, a high minimum balance and limited check writing. They again told me it sounded perfect for their needs. At that point I had my cross-sale (CD and MMDA) and was anxious to finish with them and help the next person waiting.

*Handling
Objections*

Then the husband began having second thoughts about only being able to write three checks per month on the MMDA. He became apprehensive and felt it really wouldn't be enough. He asked for "special privileges." He said something like, "I'll only need to write six or seven. I'm sure your bank can waive the penalties. My wife and I will be good customers."

I agreed that six or seven was very little and indicated that I wished I could do something for him. I asked if he presently had a regular checking account with his old bank in Connecticut. He said, "Yes" but they both felt they'd like to keep it.

Now understand that I had a lobby full of people trying to get my attention. They had read all the various magazines available and were looking at their watches, wondering just how much longer

I was going to be (in the back of my mind I shared their concern). Should I not spend time with my present customers and risk loosing multiple sales? Worse yet, should I risk giving the customers an account they don't really need? So I made a decision.

"Excuse me," I said, scooting my chair out and walking to my door. "I've got some restless people out there and I just want to let them know I will be with them soon. Now I don't want you two to leave until I have been able to help you in every way possible. Just one second."

So then I walked out to the five customers and apologized for the delay. I told them I would be with them in just five more minutes. They felt better. More important, I felt better.

When I returned to my office, I felt that the couple respected what I had just done. They made a cute comment on my juggling act and we shared polite chuckles. I asked them if they paid any service charges on their checking account in Connecticut. They said they did if their balance dropped below a certain minimum.

Ask Selling

"Mr. Smith," I asked. "You indicated to me that you're retired. Is that correct?"

He confirmed that, so I asked if he would be interested in a checking account that would have no service charges and require no minimum balance. Obviously he was interested but wondered what that had to do with his CD.

It was then that I really focused in on where I was going. "Mr. and Mrs. Smith," I said, "you are concerned that you're going to write more than three checks per month with your MMDA. Yet you want the higher interest provided by that checking account. Is that right?"

"Yes. That appears to be our problem," he stated.

"Yet you want to keep your checking account in Connecticut that you pay service charges and have to keep a minimum balance. Right?"

"We feel comfortable with that bank. We've done business with them for years. "

"I can understand that. I'd hate to loose valuable customers like yourself, too. But If I can show you a way to keep the high interest in your MMDA and eliminate all service charges and minimum balances, would you be willing to move your checking account to us?"

"Well, under those conditions, I would think so. "

Closing the Sale   I let them know that there are no service charges or minimum balances required on our 60 Plus NOW Account and that they would earn interest on any balance they keep. I explained how the interest from their CD would automatically be deposited into their high interest MMDA and any time that they wanted to transfer money on which to write checks they could move money from their MMDA to their 60 Plus NOW Account. I even drew a small diagram for them. The Smiths liked that and were ready to sign the necessary paperwork involved. *(Match Related Products to Needs!)* I started to think what a great cross-sell this is turning out to be. I suggested direct deposit of their Social Security/pension checks. They said that their checks were still going to the bank in Connecticut. I told them that it was no problem for me to fill out the forms to have the deposit transferred here.

As I was filling out the required forms, I mentioned that they could have an ATM 24-hour teller card for their NOW account. *(Handling Objections)* They tell me they are too old to use an ATM and prefer to do their banking the old fashioned way. Computers are too confusing for them. I countered that objection with a statement about my own grandparents who thought the same thing, but after learning how to use it, love it! I am a great believer in ATMs and explained all the advantages (especially the fact that they can use their ATM card to transfer money from their MMDA to their 60 Plus NOW) and then I offered to give them a demonstration to show how easy it really is. I even told them that if they don't like it, they could cut up the card and throw it away. The Smiths finally agreed and took the cards.

By now, the Smiths had been in my office for quite some time. the better part of fifteen minutes. I don't mind—the people in the lobby do. I introduce the Smiths to the tellers and ask one of my tellers to give them a demonstration for me. (*Customer Cultivation*) I thank the Smiths for coming and offer them my assistance in the future.

Follow Up

With all our new accounts the CRT generates a thank you letter. Included in the letter is a statement that says I am enclosing some information about a product or a service that they may be interested in. If I haven't had time to sell overdraft protection, I send that out in the letter. The Smiths probably don't need it, but I send it out anyway along with a brochure promoting financial management.

A couple of days later the CD promotion is over (thankfully!!!) and I see the Smiths coming into the bank. (*Customer Cultivation*) They do some business at the teller window and then ask if they may come into my office. Mrs. Smith tells me how much she loved getting the thank you letter; it made her feel like a big shot! Such personal service from someone they just met. Mr. Smith starts to tell me about the problems they are having with their condo and I commiserate with them. I notice that Mr. Smith has the overdraft application with him, so I ask what he thinks of the service. His answer is that if I think they should have it, they want it. I explain to them both that, chances are, they'll never need it but you only pay for it if you use it. How much easier can this get?

This is one of my best sells. Starting out with a CD, to a MMDA, to a NOW account, direct deposit, ATM cards and overdraft protection. This looks terrific on my tracking sheets!!! I realize that with some time and effort, each customer can be a cross-sell.

Case Study #2

What a great cup of coffee! I really enjoy these few quiet moments at my desk, alone with my coffee and my thoughts. It's a super way to begin a productive day! Once the bank doors open, I can never count on anything to be routine. Aaaah, but I guess I wouldn't have it any other way!

I really enjoy the branch I work at. It is located in what you might call a "yuppy/dink" (*Double Income No Kids*) neighborhood. Most of my customers are in their mid-30s, drive fancy cars, wear the latest trends, eat microwave dinners, and are forever traveling. Some are married, some are not, but they have one thing in common—THEY ARE MONEY SPEND-ERS.

Introduction

Uh-oh! There's goes my tranquility. The doors have opened and the day has begun. A customer is approaching my desk now. I look up, stand up, and extend my hand in welcome. *(Customer Greeting)*

"Good Morning, I am Jane Wilson. Won't you please have a seat."

The customer sits down in the seat adjacent to my desk. "Thank you," he says. "My name is Jon Jones and I am interested in a loan for a living room set." *(Product Inquiry)*

"I'll be happy to help you with your loan needs, Mr. Jones."

"Please call me Jon."

"Thank you. I'm Jane. So, you're shopping for a living room set. Did you just move to the area?" *(Question/Question)*

Needs Analysis

"Yes, just last week. I moved into the condos right across the street."

"What brings you to Connecticut?" I ask as I continue to take notes. *(Personal Questioning)*

"A new job with an insurance company," Jon says.

Direct Question

"Is this your first time to Connecticut, Jon?"

"Second, the first time was for my interview."

Open-Ended
Question

"What do you like most about our state?"
"Coming from Colorado, I'd have to say the ocean. I really enjoy water sports and have already been to the beach. One of the guys at work is into windsurfing so he's going to teach me the ropes. Who knows, if I make enough money at work, maybe I'll buy a condo on the water!"

"My husband and I love the water. We've found the New England summers great for so many activities. I've never been to Colorado, Jon, except flying into the airport once. I saw the mountains. That was about it. Tell me about Colorado. You think I'd like it? (Open-ended Question) A smile comes to his face."

"Colorado will always be my home. I was born there and will probably return one day. There's a magic about the mountains that's hard to describe. The air is different there. Cleaner, I think. With all my family there, I will always have an 'excuse' to visit. I could talk about Colorado for a long time."

"It must have been very difficult to leave to come to Connecticut. I sure hope our state can make you feel as good. It is very beautiful, too, and fun to explore. Do you like to travel?" I ask. (Direct Question)

"Not in the sense that some people do. I'm into antiques and travel around looking for antiques . . . rather than travel for the sake of sight seeing. I know that New England is a real magnet for antique hunters. I'm looking forward to traveling to some of those quaint old New England antique shops."

"Jon, if you're looking for a loan, have you, by any chance, established an account relationship with us?" *(Matching Related Products to Needs)*

"You mean a checking account?"

"Actually any account."

"No. Do I need to?"

"I just think it would be easier for you. Do you have a checking account in Connecticut?"

"Not yet. I haven't been paid yet. Thought I'd wait till then."

Needs Fulfillment   "Well, you can wait but it might be easier getting approval for that loan if you are an existing customer. More important, it will be easier for you since we can automatically make payments on the loan from your checking account."

"How does that work?"

"The bank automatically takes the amount of your loan payment from your checking account and makes the payment for you."

"Banks can do that?"

"They sure can. That's how I remember to make my car payments each month."

"Uhmm. Makes sense. So I'll open a checking account and bring you my paycheck at the end of the month."

"I think we can make it easier on you."

"How's that?"

"Your employer can automatically send your paycheck here every month for direct deposit into your checking account. Your loan on your furniture will automatically be paid, also. I don't know how serious you are about antiques but, depending on your level of commitment and your paycheck, you can build a nest egg through forced savings. I mention that now only because it might be easier to do every thing all at once."

"You mean automatically save up for antiques?"

"Exactly. How much do you think you could put away?"

Handling Objections

"Well. I don't know. You're going a little fast for me. I'm gonna have to think about that. I will open up the checking account, though. Especially if it will help getting my loan approved."

"That's fine, Jon." I realized at that point I had gone too far. It was too early to go into a savings plan. Maybe I've lost his level of trust. I'd better be careful.

"If you'll fill out this loan application, I'll open up your checking account and get you a number. How much can you put into the new account today?" *(Call to Action)*

"Well, let's see," he said rummaging through his billfold. I have a check here for $800. And I'm walking around with at least $500 in cash. Let's start with $1,300."

"That will be fine, Jon. Sign here and here for your checking account. And sign here for your ATM card. Your new ATM card is standard equipment on all our checking accounts. They're free. It will allow you 24-hour access to our teller machines, or to ATM machines throughout New England. That should be pretty handy if you're antiquing out of town and can't resist the impulse. With this checking account opened I think I can get back to you this afternoon on your loan. Where can I reach you, say, mid-afternoon?"

Call Back

"Here's my new business card. I should be in my office all afternoon."

Follow Up

As Jon leaves my office, I pull out a thank you card to send him and jot down information for future reference on a 3 x 5 card for my customer information box. "I read somewhere about an antique show in Sturbridge. I wonder where I put that information. I must remember to send it to Jon," I tell myself.

Case Study #3

Background

I have enjoyed sales relationships with up-scale customers, particularly in the area of financial advice in conjunction with normal retail sales activity. The following case study should illustrate that sales situation. It is said that Washington's Birthday is the busiest car sale day of the year. Invariably I will have a customer who comes in the week prior to that holiday to get him or herself prepared to buy a car.

The customer is approaching my desk. I know her. Her name is Stephanie Hollis. I know her well enough to call her "Stevey." She is a fairly regular customer of the bank. I know she has a checking account and ATM with the bank. She came to me for a mortgage when she purchased a condo nearby. I remember because it was such a good deal and in the process I remember being impressed with the kind of money she was making as a product manager for a computer company.

Pre-Sales Planning

Luckily, I wrote this all down on a card in the little recipe box that holds relevant sales information on certain clients. And, as I am wont to do when I spot familiar customers, I quickly pulled Stevey's index card and scan it while she approached my desk.

Introduction   "Stevey," I say, standing at my desk. "How're you doing?"

"Just fine. You got a couple of minutes?"

"I sure do."

"I'm trying to figure out the best way to buy a car I found."

"Why don't you let Jackson Instruments buy it for you?"

"I've already thought of that. The word through the grapevine is that I would be the only product manager with a company car. They'd nix that. So I don't want to make an issue of it."

"Do you really need a new car or have you just fallen in love?"

"I really need a car." Then she smiled. "AND I've fallen in love."

Financial Question "Uh oh. That's trouble. There goes the budget." We both laugh.

"How much?"

"They're asking 21."

"Twenty-one hundred?" I ask, smirking.

"Twenty-one thousand."

"Why don't you buy it?"

"I am. That's why I'm here. What are your rates?"

"I don't know if they're competitive with dealer's rates. Let's see." I pull the rate sheet out of my top drawer. "We're at 9.87. What are their rates?"

"I'm not buying from a dealer. I'm buying this privately."

"You're buying a used car? What are you buying?"

"A two-year-old BMW convertible. Fifty-two hundred miles. Not a scratch on it."

"Stevey, 9.87 is our new car rate. You're talking 12.9% for used cars."

"Wow!! 12.9%!! How much is that per month?"

"Well, the most we can loan you on a two-year-old BMW is $17,000," I said looking through my book and then flipping to the monthly calculations. "And that would cost you $456.00 per month."

"I can't afford that."

Needs Analysis

"Stevey. How do you like your condo?" *(Ask Selling)*

"Why are you trying to change the subject?"

"Actually, I'm not. Let's see, how long have you owned that condo?"

"Just about five years, but what's that got to do with a new car?"

"A lot. What did you pay for your condo?"

"About ninety thousand."

"And what's it worth today . . . hundred and ten or twenty?"

"Probably. Maybe more. My next door neighbor's place just went for one-thirty-six. Are you suggesting I re-mortgage . . . just for a BMW?"

"Not at all. What would you say if I could offer you a way to buy that BMW for eight percent? Would you be interested?"

"Of course, I would. Can you?"

Needs Fulfillment "I think so," I said. Then I explained to her about the bank's Equity Credit Line; how you write checks based on what you need and pay interest only on what you spend. Stevey was very interested. Then she confided in me on her "fall back" position.

" . . . I could just wait 'till the end of the year and use my bonus to pay for it but I'm afraid I won't get another deal like this. It's a great car."

"Stevey, I don't know a great BMW from a '62 Ford Falcon. You know, this might be the time to look at your financial picture and figure out cost-effective ways to allow you the kind of purchasing power that you've accrued."

"You mean get my car even cheaper?"

"Actually I'm thinking about your next car or your next living room suite or your kids' college education . . ."

"Hold it, JoAnn. I'm not even married yet."

"I'm talking about financial planning, Stevey. If you start doing it right, at this point, it will make major financial decisions easier in the future."

"Like what?"

Follow Up

"You make a pretty good salary. You're single. You own your own condo. Your absolutely necessary expenses aren't that great. Your income taxes are probably horrendous. Have you ever though about using your present financial status to develop and insure your future financial security?"

"You mean do I invest in the stock market? The answer is no. I don't know anything about it."

"Well, I don't mean the stock market, exactly. I mean directing a certain amount of money regularly into low risk investments that will always return money to you. Some stocks are low risk. Some are extremely high risk and you could lose everything. Mutual Funds are low to medium risk . . . depending on the fund. Certificates are low risk and guaranteed . . . but they are also low return. My point here, Stevey, is this. I am not a Certified Financial Planner. That's a title that takes about two years of schooling to earn but I am interested in financial planning and the bank is training me. We have professionals on our staff who do this kind of thing. I'd like to sit you down with one and in addition to solving your BMW crisis, do some solid financial planning for the future. Would you be interested in that?"

"Absolutely. But I'd like to get the car right away. Today."

"I know. I'm sure that we can do that. "

"You mean I can get an Equity Credit Line today?"

"No. That will take two weeks. And you're telling me you don't want to wait, right?"

"Right. "

"Well. I can give you another loan until the Credit Line comes through. Then we'll pay off the short-term loan with the Credit Line."

"And I'll pay the 12 or 13 percent while I'm waiting."

"I don't think so. I think I might be able to get you the prime rate plus a couple of points . . . which is about the same as our Equity Credit Line. You'll probably need it for sixty days . . . just to be safe. You can pay it off before then."

"I can do that today?"

"Either this afternoon or first thing in the morning. We just need to fill out some applications. Have you got another half hour?"

"If I can call and tell them I'm taking the car, I've got all the time you need."

"Great. And then I'll arrange for you, me and our Certified Financial Planner to

have an exploratory meeting. What is a
good time for you next week?"

I was very careful not to promise anything. I did, however,
assure my client that I felt I could get the loan and the money. I
did so because I was familiar with her background. I had re-fa-
miliarized myself with her status by way of my card file. I called
up her account status on my computer. I know that she had a
checking account. She always maintained an adequate minimum balance. Never had overdrawn. Has an ATM card and
uses it frequently. Has $4,000 in a one-year CD. And, she has a
$76,000 mortgage with us.

Stevey was a prime candidate for financial planning. The
opportunity came about indirectly. I find most opportunities for
financial planning come that way. Consumers don't walk into
banks expecting detailed financial planning. Most retail banking
customers come in expecting a specific product or service. To
date, financial planning is not one of those services. However, I
do feel that will change in the near future.

INDEX

selection, 38, 43-44
Law firs, 7
Lead product, 143, 161, 163, 165
  concept, 177
  identification, 159-162
  sales, 177
  sales path, 163, 183
  selling, 181, 188
    non-retail, 191-198
    retail, 157-189
  services, visualization, 162-163
Lease, *see* Net
Legal
  assistance, 4
  holder, 4
  services, 6
Lending authority, 171
Letters of credit, 161
Liability, *see* Tax
Liability-based product, 171
Life insurance, *see* Savings
Liquidity, 43
Listen/apologize/explore/resp
  ond (LAER), 31, 33
Listening, 52, 54, 75
  techniques, 77
Loans, 4, 160, 170, 227, 229, 230
  see Commercial, Installment
  applications, 102, 171
  payment, 229
Long-range investment vehicles,
  148
Long-term stock funds, 149, 154
Lyrics, 38, 43-44
  see Organization, Topics

M

Managers, *see* Sales
Manual, *see* Product
Marketing
  department, 99
  point of view, 191
  process, 147
Maslow, Theory of Hierarchy,
  187
Match related products, 117, 224,
  229
Maturity, 168
MMA, *see* Money
MMDA, 170, 221, 224, 226
Momentum questions, 67, 69, 74,
  76
Money
  see New, Transferred
  market accounts (MMA), 52,
  161, 170, 213, 220
Mortgage(s), 4, 6, 232
  see Bi-monthly
  bond funds, 150
  rate, 175
Mortgage-backed securities, 150,
  155
Multiple
  product sales, 174, 177
  sales, 222
Municipal bonds, 150
Music, 38, 43
  see Rate, Volume
Mutual fund, 6, 7, 112, 117, 134,
  147, 148, 161, 175, 187, 191,
  236

style, 32, 49
Personnel, *see* Platform
Physical
  contact, 38, 40-41
  professionalism, 42
Pitch, 48
Platform personnel, 114
Posture, 38, 41
Pre-approach planning, 12, 14, 16
Pre-closing, 122
Preparation
  see Sales model
  stage, 131
Pre-sales planning, 83, 84, 113, 218, 219, 232-233
Presentations, 134
Primacy, 47, 48
  recency comparison, 44-46
Probe, 158, 178, 180
  see Closed, Open, Verification
Probing process, 122
Problem resolution, 30
Product
  see Bank, Banking, Cross-sold, Lead, Liability-based, Match, Multiple, Relationship
  diagrams, 99
  forms, 83
  information, 83
  manual, 99
  inquiry, 72, 113, 114, 219, 227
  knowledge, 208
  manager, 232, 233
  manuals, 84, 99, 132
  sale, 30

value, 178-179
Productivity, 27, 137, 141
  see Sales
Promotions, 134
Proposals, 134

Q

Question, 158
  see Direct, Financial, Momentum, Open-ended, Trial
Questioning, 51-76, 167
  see Financial, Personal, Personal/financial
  intensity curves, 57-63
  process, 115
  skills, 115
  stages, 55-57
Question/question, 68, 71, 72, 113, 115, 178, 193, 227
  techniques, 175

R

Rate (music), 38, 43
Rate(s), 99
  sheets, *see* Competitive, Competitor
Recency, primacy comparison, 44-46
Referral, 84
  see Internal
Re-grouping, 67, 68, 74, 76, 119
Rejection, 125, 134
  see Sales
Relationship, 166
  see Banking, Customer, Direct
  activity, 232